A CONCISE
BIBLE
SURVEY

TRACING THE PROMISES OF GOD

CHRISTOPHER CONE

A Concise Bible Survey: Tracing the Promises of God

4th Edition 2012

©2012 Christopher Cone

Exegetica Publishing

Ft. Worth, TX

1st-3rd Edition's published as The Promises of God: A Synthetic Bible Survey

ISBN-10: 0976593033

ISBN-13: 978-0-9765930-3-4

All Scripture quotations, except those noted otherwise are from the New American Standard Bible, ©1960,1962,1963,1968,1971,1972,1973,1975, and 1977 by the Lockman Foundation.

Studying the Bible is like studying the forest and the trees. Exegesis examines the detail of every leaf.

Systematic theology categorizes every kind of tree.

Synthetic survey takes a bird's eye view of the whole forest. Without that broad perspective, we don't know where the leaves fit, and we can't begin to fathom how many different kinds of trees there really are.

Can you see the forest from the trees?

Enjoy the forest...

Affectionately dedicated to

My cherished Cathy – Thank you for who you are to me, and for making this possible. Your love for the Lord brings me joy. Many have done nobly, but you excel them all.

I love you.

and

My adored Christiana & Cara Grace– I pray that this will help you both as you seek His face. I hope that it adds to your joy in studying His Word, and that through it, in some small way, I may pass along to you an example of His love, as my blessed parents have tirelessly done for me. I love you.

With special thanks to

Ralph, Lucy and KC Cone,

When I glance at the pages of Scripture, I am reminded of your gift to me. You taught me to love the Lord and to cherish His word. There is no greater gift that parents and a brother could have given. My heart has been shaped by your examples and by your love. I only pray that I could be such a blessed influence to others. I owe you a debt of love.

Table of Contents

Introduction

The Bible is an amazing book. It has been circulated more, read more, and discussed more than any other book in all of history. But it is more than just a book. It is more than just a compilation of stories and narratives and morals and poems. God's word is an orderly communication of Himself, and to specific ends. God seeks to be known. After all, John 17:3 tells us that the true meaning of life – even the very definition of life – is to know God. The Bible, therefore, is God's revelation of Himself to mankind, in order that His character may be clearly demonstrated, seen, and to whatever degree He desires, understood.

We are told that all Scripture is God-breathed (2 Tim. 3:16). Consequently the value of examining the words of Scripture is great, for they are *His* words – His own accounting of Himself and His plan. His creative work is evident to all, and much of His character and person can be seen in creation itself. As the Psalmist says, "the heavens are telling of the glory of God" (Ps. 19:1). But yet, He has graciously given us so much more than even the artful creation before us. He has graced us with the His word of truth, that which is useful for teaching, for reproof, for correction, for training in righteousness. For how shall we come to Him if we are not told of Him, and who shall tell us of Him if He does not tell us Himself? But He does tell us.   And just as in creation we see patterns and organization, we see the same themes of sovereignty, holiness, and grandeur running throughout the Bible.

Connecting these themes is an important thread running through the entire Scriptures. That thread is a key to understanding Scripture as one clear and cohesive message. It guides us from the opening words of Genesis to the closing *Amen* of Revelation, and ties them together so beautifully that it is evident that only God could be the author of such an incredibly divine symphony of life.

God's promises and the fulfillment of those promises provide the basic structure and outline of God's communication with man in the Bible. Not only does a Bible survey based on the promises of God give us an outline of Scripture, but it also provides an outline of world history itself - including past, present, and future. Through understanding the promises of God, we get a glimpse of the glory of the covenant-keeping God.

> *Many other signs therefore Jesus also performed in the presence of the disciples which are not written in this book; but these have been written that you may believe that Jesus is the Christ, the Son of God; and that believing you may have life in His name.*
>
> *John 20:30-31*

Meaning of *Bible*: From the Greek singular noun *biblos*, referred to the 11th century use in Egypt of the outer surface of a papyrus reed for writing. Christians later used the plural *biblia* to describe their writings as early as 100AD. This term was transliterated into Old French, and later, modern English.

1

Promises Previewed

The Chronology of the Hebrew Bible

The books of the Hebrew Bible can be categorized into four different categories: Chronological, Complementary, Wisdom, and Prophetic.

CHRONOLOGICAL BOOKS - There are eleven such books, forming the backbone of the Hebrew Bible, covering 3600 years in chronological order. One leads into the next, and read one after the other, they cover the entire chronology of the Hebrew Bible.

Genesis – (4004-1900) – creation, Noah, Abraham, Isaac, Jacob, and Joseph.

Exodus – (1525-1440) – the conclusion of Israel's enslavement in Egypt, the Exodus, and the Mosaic Covenant.

Numbers – (1440-1400) – Israel's 40 years in the wilderness, the two numberings, one before the wandering, one after.

Joshua – (1400-1370) – Israel's swift, yet incomplete conquest of Canaan.

Judges – (1370-1050) – covers the years that judges ruled Israel.

1 Samuel – (1100-1011) – the call of Samuel, the reign of Saul, and the early life of David.

2 Samuel – (1011-971) – the reign of David as king over Israel.

1 and 2 Kings – (971-586) – Solomon's kingdom, the divided kingdom, and the beginning of the exile.

Ezra – (538-450) – the spiritual restoration of Israel from the exile.

Nehemiah – (445-433) – the political restoration of Israel from the exile, and chronologically ends the Old Testament.

COMPLEMENTARY BOOKS – They contain historical accounts, and cover time periods contemporary to the Chronological Books.

The events of **Job** occur during the time of Genesis.

Leviticus is contemporary to Exodus.

Deuteronomy records the second giving of the Law occurring chronologically in the book of Numbers.

Ruth lived during the times of the judges.

1 Chronicles covers the events of 2 Samuel from a priestly perspective.

2 Chronicles deals with the events of 1 and 2 Kings from a priestly perspective.

The events of **Esther** took place after the exile.

WISDOM BOOKS – These books were written or compiled primarily during the Monarchy and Divided Kingdom.

Psalms – written primarily by David, some by Asaph, Moses, Solomon, and others.

Proverbs – wisdom verses primarily from the pen of Solomon.

Ecclesiastes – an examination by Solomon of the meaning of life.

Song of Solomon – a portrait of marital love, also by Solomon.

PROPHETIC BOOKS – five groups of prophetic books written during the Monarchy, Divided Kingdom, and Exile:

A. Prophets to the Nations

>**Obadiah** (840) – message of judgment to Edom.
>
>**Jonah** (780) – a call for repentance to Ninevah.
>
>**Nahum** (650-612) – oracle of judgment against Ninevah.

B. Prophets to the Northern Kingdom of Israel

>**Amos** (755) – judgment, a call to repentance, and promise of future restoration.
>
>**Hosea** (750) – a vivid portrait of God's love toward Israel, despite her unfaithfulness.

C. Prophets to the Southern Kingdom of Judah

Joel (835) – judgment, deliverance, the Day of the Lord, and future blessing.

Micah (725) – judgment on the North and South, rebuke of the leaders, and future hope.

Isaiah (740-680) – the rejection and restoration of Israel by God, and the coming of Messiah.

Zephaniah (625) – the Day of the Lord: a day of wrath, and a day of restoration.

Habakkuk (609) – questions of God's sovereignty in dealing with Israel.

Jeremiah (627-586) – final pronouncements of judgment, promises of future blessing.

D. Prophets during the Exile

Lamentations (586) – Jeremiah's mourning over the fall of Jerusalem.

Ezekiel (593-570) – the sovereignty of God, judgment on Israel, and the future hope of the Kingdom.

Daniel (536) – God's deliverance of His people, and the timelines.

E. Prophets during the Restoration

Haggai (520) – encouragement to complete the temple.

Zechariah (520-518) – visions, messages, and burdens of hope and redemption for Israel.

Malachi (450-400) – rebuke of priests, and promise of the forerunner.

*The Hebrew Bible**

1. The Torah (Law):
    Genesis, Exodus, Leviticus, Numbers,
    Deuteronomy

2. The Nevi'im (Prophets):
    A. The Former: Joshua, Judges, Samuel,
    Kings
    B. The Latter: Isaiah, Jeremiah, Ezekiel,
    The Twelve (Hosea, Joel, Amos, Obadiah,
    Jonah, Micah, Nahum, Habakkuk,
    Zephaniah, Haggai, Zechariah, Malachi)

3. The Ketuvim (Writings):
    A. Psalms, Proverbs, Job
    B. Megillot (Scrolls): Song of Solomon,
    Ruth, Lamentations, Ecclesiastes, Esther
    C. Daniel, Ezra-Nehemiah, Chronicles

*Collectively referred to as the TaNaK, an acronym of the
three sections.

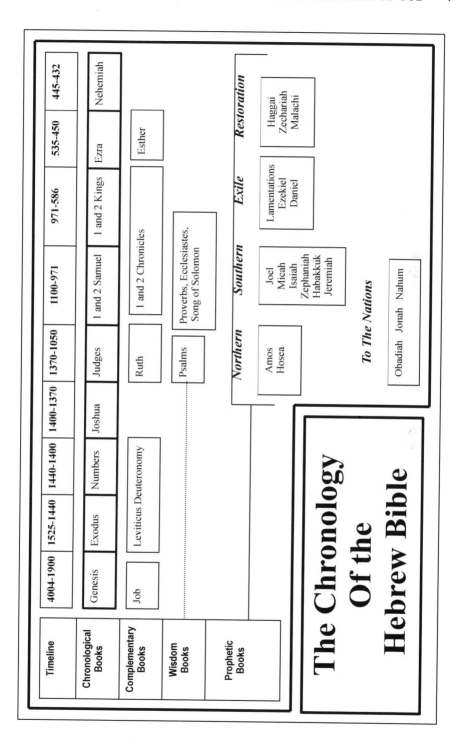

The Chronology
Of the
Hebrew Bible

Timeline	4004-1900	1525-1440	1440-1400	1400-1370	1370-1050	1100-971	971-586	535-450	445-432
Chronological Books	Genesis	Exodus	Numbers	Joshua	Judges	1 and 2 Samuel	1 and 2 Kings	Ezra	Nehemiah
Complementary Books		Leviticus Deuteronomy			Ruth	1 and 2 Chronicles		Esther	
Wisdom Books	Job				Psalms	Proverbs, Ecclesiastes, Song of Solomon			
Prophetic Books									

Northern   Southern   Exile   Restoration

Amos
Hosea

Joel
Micah
Isaiah
Zephaniah
Habakkuk
Jeremiah

Lamentations
Ezekiel
Daniel

Haggai
Zechariah
Malachi

To The Nations

Obadiah   Jonah   Nahum

2

Promises Made

Conscience and Theocracy

4004-1370 BC
Chronological Books

Genesis 4004-1900 BC	Exodus 1525-1440 BC	Numbers 1440-1400 BC	Joshua 1400-1370 BC

Complementary Books

Job	Leviticus	Deuteronomy

Key Promises

The First Promise: The Need For Redemption ----------Gen. 2:15-17

The Redemptive Promise: Suffering Messiah ---------Gen. 3:15 (3:21; 4:1,25)

The Noahic Covenant ------------------------------Gen. 8:21-9:17 (6:5-8)

The Abrahamic Covenant--------------------Gen. 12:1-3, 15:3-21 (45:5)

The Egyptian Exile and Exodus--------------Gen. 15:13-14 (45:5); Ex. 6:2-8; 12:12-13,40

The Land Covenant ------------------ Gen. 15:18-21; Deut 30, Josh 24

Regarding Ishmael ------------------Gen. 16:10-14, 21:9-21 (17:17-21)

Regarding Isaac ---Gen. 17:17-21

Regarding Jacob and Esau ------------------------------Gen. 25:22-23

To Jacob--Gen. 28:10-17 (49:10)

Regarding Judah: Tribe of Royalty ----------------------Gen. 49:10

The Mosaic Covenant --------------------------------------Ex 20-24

The Wilderness Exile ----------------------------------Num. 14:28-35

The Exile From the Promised Land----------Lev. 25:1-4; 26:1-46;
Deut. 28-30 (9:4,6) (15:4-5,11)

Failed Conquest --Josh. 23:11-13

GENESIS   4004-1800 BC

Creation	The Fall	Abel, Cain & Seth	Noah & The Flood	The Tower Of Babel	To Abraham	To Isaac	To Jacob	To Joseph
1-2	3	4	5-10	11	12-25:11	25:12-27:46	28-36	37-50

Genesis: God Relates To Man

Key Promises

The First Promise: The Need for Redemption -----------Gen. 2:15-17

The Redemptive Promise: A Suffering Messiah --------------Gen. 3:15

The Noahic Covenant --Gen. 8:21-9:17

The Abrahamic Covenant ----------------------------Gen. 12:1-3; 15:3-21

The Egyptian Exile and Exodus ---------------------------Gen. 15:13-14

The Land Covenant ---Gen. 15:18-21

Regarding Ishmael --------------------------------Gen. 16:10-14; 21:9-21

Regarding Isaac --Gen. 17:17-21

Regarding Jacob and Esau ----------------------------------Gen. 25:22-23

To Jacob --Gen. 28:10-17

Regarding Judah: Tribe of Royalty----------------------------Gen. 49:10

Title

The Hebrew title of the book is *bereshith* (the first word in the Hebrew text), meaning *in the beginning. Genesis* is from the Latin translation of this word and is also related to the Greek root *genos,* referring to lineage and beginnings.

Authorship

Moses' authorship of the Torah (or Pentateuch - the first five books of the Bible) is affirmed throughout Scripture. The Biblical interpreter using the literal grammatical-historical interpretive method will conclude that Moses was indeed the author.

There are numerous claims within the Torah of Mosaic authorship[1] as well as other Hebrew Bible books containing statements to the same effect.[2] Further, Christ Himself identified Moses as the writer of the first five books on more than fifteen recorded occasions.[3] Most significantly in Luke 24:44 He refers to the entire Hebrew Bible, divided as the Jews of that day recognized into three categories: "the Law of Moses and the Prophets, and the Psalms."

Only in recent years has Mosaic authorship of these books been challenged and most notably so by Julius Wellhausen (1844-1918). Wellhausen argued for the Documentary Theory, also known as the JEDP theory – a theory that suggested several men as being responsible for the authorship of the Torah:

"J" is for "Jahwist," as this supposed author seemed to prefer to use the name Jehovah (in Hebrew, *Yahweh*) for God. This author wrote in approximately 850 BC.

"E" is for "Elohist," as this author penned the Hebrew word *Elohim* when referring to God. He wrote around 750 BC.

"D" is for "Deuteronomist," the unnamed redactor of 650 BC who edited and combined documents "J" and "E," arriving at the deuteronomic account.

"P" is for the "Priestly" author, primarily of Leviticus, but of other priestly and institutional sections as well.

This form of criticism assumes that because there are variances in the writing 'style' and because there is found within these books a very broad range of subjects, time, and information covered, that it could not possibly be the work of just one author, and the theory dismisses completely the idea of God's inspiring and revealing work.

While Wellhausen was not the primary originator of this theory, he seemed to be it's loudest defender. And the issue at stake is not simply the question of who wrote these books. The process by which Wellhausen and others arrive at their conclusions is a dangerous one, as Gleason Archer points out:

> The Documentary Theory has been characterized by a subtle species of circular reasoning; it tends to posit its conclusion (the Bible is no supernatural revelation) as its underlying premise (there can be no such thing as supernatural revelation)...Unfortunately...it rendered impossible any fair consideration of the evidences presented by the Scripture of supernatural revelation. Furthermore, it made it absolutely obligatory to find rationalistic, humanistic explanations of every miraculous or God-manifesting feature or episode in the text of Scripture.[4]

It is imperative for the Bible student to recognize the conflict between Biblical claims and the claims of liberal criticism. They are mutually exclusive. As a result, we must make a choice to either acknowledge God's sovereign and supernatural work in revealing Himself or to thoroughly discount it.

But again, despite any lack of clarity in the arguments or intentions of the critics of Mosaic authorship, the Bible stands clear in its testimony that Moses was the mouthpiece chosen by God to pen the Torah.

Structure

In addition to the topical divisions of Genesis (as shown in the outline chart) the book is also divided into twelve sections, each one (except for the first) beginning with the Hebrew word *toledoth* (*the generations of*). The *toledoth* divisions are as follows:

1. Creation 1:1 - 2:3 (no *toledoth* introduction)
2. The account of the heavens and the earth 2:4 - 4:26
3. The book of the genealogy of Adam 5:1 - 6:8
4. The genealogy of Noah 6:9 - 9:29
5. The genealogy of the sons of Noah 10:1 -11:9
6. The genealogy of Shem 11:10-26
7. The genealogy of Terah (Abraham) 11:27 - 25:11
8. The genealogy of Ishmael 25:12-18
9. The genealogy of Isaac 25:19 - 35:29
10. The genealogy of Esau 36:1-8
11. The genealogy of the sons of Esau 36:9-43
12. The genealogy of Jacob 37:1 - 50:26

Genesis 1 -11
God Relates to Man in General

The first eleven chapters of Genesis give us the account of God's dealings with mankind in general. Throughout these first chapters, we see God beginning to hone in on specific people through whom He will work His master plan. Genesis 1-2 records the account of creation, and chapter two is highlighted by God's first promise to man:

> And the Lord God commanded the man saying, 'From any tree of the garden you may eat freely; but from the tree of the knowledge of good and evil you shall not eat, for in the day that you eat from it you shall surely die' (2:16-17).

At this early stage in history Adam and Eve had life – they knew God intimately and had a beautiful fellowship with Him. That fellowship was to be maintained and protected simply by obeying one imperative.

Genesis 3 gives us the account of Adam and Eve's failure to keep this command. The consequence was death – immediate spiritual death, and eventual physical death. God had kept His first promise. Mankind was immediately separated from fellowship with God – further demonstrated by God when He banished the first couple from the Garden of Eden. The fellowship was irrevocably destroyed, and man had no ability to correct it. But even in the tragedy of God's pronounced judgment, He made another promise:

> And I will put enmity between you [the serpent] and the woman, and between your seed and her seed; He shall bruise you on the head, and you shall bruise Him on the heel (3:15).

As God pronounced judgment on the serpent (Satan, see Rev. 12:9; 20:2), He declared that the seed of woman would execute this very judgment. Note that *seed* here is singular – it references a specific descendant. It later becomes evident that this promise would provide the means to restore the fellowship between God and His created beings. With each promise made in Scripture, God's plan becomes clearer. In the beginning, the promises seem vague and somewhat mysterious, but as Scripture progresses we find the promises explicitly specific.

Genesis 4 records the tragic murder of Abel by his brother Cain, and again – even as God is judging the wickedness of Cain He makes another promise of deliverance, this one specifically for Cain (4:15). Genesis 5 gives us the record of the descendants of Adam through Noah – the next man to whom God would make a promise. Genesis 6 begins with God's lament over what mankind had become:

> Then the Lord saw that the wickedness of man was great on the earth, and that every intent of the thoughts of his heart was only evil continually (6:5).

The evil on earth had become so great that God would no longer tolerate it. He could perhaps have blotted out mankind entirely and started over – but remember, He had made a promise of deliverance (3:15) that He must keep. God keeps His promises, so God chose a man through whom the thread would continue. That man was Noah.

God's promises do not fail. Even though God would judge mankind by flood, He kept His promise. Genesis 7-8 records the events of the flood and how God remembered the righteousness of Noah, and how He used Noah to save a remnant of the human race, in order to keep His promise.   In Genesis 8 God makes another promise, this one to Noah. The Noahic Covenant is comprised of two parts:

First is the element of the promise that God made to Himself:

> And the Lord said to Himself, 'I will never again curse the ground on account of man, for the intent of man's heart is evil from his youth; and I will never again destroy every living thing, as I have done; while the earth remains, seedtime and harvest, and cold and heat, and summer and winter, and day and night shall not cease' (8:21b-22).

At this point we now know that God will spare human life and the continuous cycle of life until He has accomplished His purpose – which includes keeping His promises.

Second is the covenant God makes with Noah:

> '...And I establish My covenant with you; and all flesh shall never again be cut off by the water of the flood, neither shall there again be a flood to destroy the earth' (9:11).

God then refers to this covenant as an "everlasting covenant between God and every living creature of all flesh that is on the earth." Once again, God makes Himself accountable to creation by giving His word that He will not destroy the earth by flood ever again. Just ponder the grace of God: He has all the intrinsic power as the Creator and the Almighty, yet He limits (by the promises in His word) what He can and will do. This is a theme evident throughout the Bible: *God willingly limits Himself.* By His declaration that He will do one thing, He eliminates the possibility that He will do the opposite. And so it is that the Almighty God reaches down to us.

It should also be noted, if only in passing at this point, that the Noahic Covenant also includes some other significant points, including permission to eat meat (9:3-4), and a mandate for capital punishment as the consequence for murder (9:6).

Genesis 10 continues on to trace the progeny of Noah. He had three sons: Shem, Ham, and Japheth.

> These are the families of the sons of Noah, according to their genealogies, by their nations; and out of these the nations were separated on the earth after the flood (10:32).

Mankind grew numerous and mighty in unity. Genesis 11 records man's continued defiance of God:

> And they said, 'Come let us build for ourselves a city, and a tower whose top will reach into heaven, and let us make for ourselves a name; lest we be scattered abroad over the face of the whole earth' (11:4).

This was a direct violation of God's command to be fruitful and multiply and fill the earth (1:28; 9:1), and it resulted in God taking unique action once again to further His plan. Genesis 11 records the events at the Tower of Babel, where God confused man's languages and destroyed their unity, forcing them to scatter and once again submit to the will of the Almighty God.

The chapter closes with the genealogy of Shem, differing from the genealogy in chapter ten only in that it traces a specific line – the line to Abraham. It is Abraham who would be the instrument God would use to bless all of humanity and keep His promise.

The first eleven chapters of Genesis record God dealing with humanity as a whole. Even the covenant God made with Noah impacted all of creation. Up to this point, God had still not yet made it clear how or through whom He intended to keep His promise of deliverance and redemption, but it is in Genesis 12 that the outline of Scripture truly begins to take shape. Out of the shadows emerges God's grand plan of the ages.

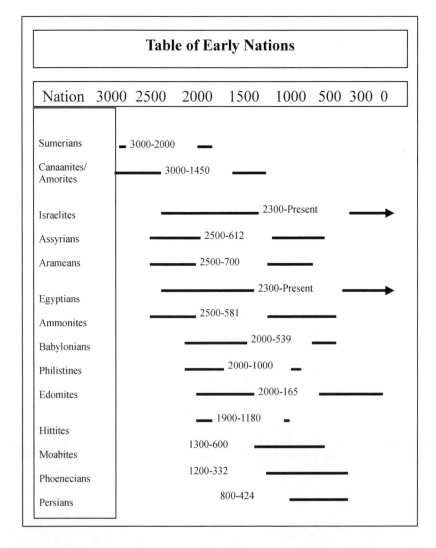

Table of Early Nations							
Nation	3000	2500	2000	1500	1000	500	300	0

Nation	Dates
Sumerians	3000-2000
Canaanites/Amorites	3000-1450
Israelites	2300-Present
Assyrians	2500-612
Arameans	2500-700
Egyptians	2300-Present
Ammonites	2500-581
Babylonians	2000-539
Philistines	2000-1000
Edomites	2000-165
Hittites	1900-1180
Moabites	1300-600
Phoenecians	1200-332
Persians	800-424

Genesis 12:1-3

The Abrahamic Covenant

If there is a single passage which provides the setting for the remainder of Scripture, it is Genesis 12:1-3, God's promise to Abraham. In the previous chapters of Genesis, God dealt with mankind on a more general basis. In chapter twelve He chooses one man and directs all of His work with mankind through one promise – the Abrahamic Covenant:

> Now the Lord said to Abram, 'Go forth from your country, and from your relatives and from your father's house, to the land I will show you; and I will make you a great nation and I will bless you, and make your name great; and so you shall be a blessing; and I will bless those who bless you, and the one who curses you I will curse. And in you all the families of the earth shall be blessed' (12:1-3).

It is important to note that while this covenant was indeed unconditional (once ratified, it was not dependent upon anyone other than God, since He instituted no conditions which could negate the promises He made), it did hinge initially upon Abraham's obedience to the imperative "Go forth from your country, and from your relatives and from your father's house to the land which I will show you." Abraham was told essentially to leave all that he had known and if he was obedient to this one thing, the covenant would be set in motion. He did, and it was.

The Abrahamic Covenant contains seven specific promises with three general elements.

The *seven promises* are:

1. I will make you a great nation.
2. I will bless you.
3. [I will] make your name great.
4. You shall be a blessing.
5. I will bless those who bless you.

6. The one who curses you I will curse.

7. In you all the families of the earth shall be blessed.

The *three general elements* are:
1. people
2. land
3. kingdom

The Promises

1. *I will make you a great nation.*

This promise requires that the three elements be in place – a nation cannot be great without people, land, and a kingdom. God's promise entailed innumerable descendants for Abraham, a splendid land (which God would show him), and what would ultimately be an eternal kingdom.

2. *I will bless you.*

The promises were not general as God's promises were previously. Rather than being aimed at mankind as a whole, this promise was directed at a specific individual.

3. *[I will] make your name great.*

The blessing upon Abraham would be so magnificent that his name would be highly regarded and meaningful in the ages to come.

4. *You shall be a blessing.*

Not only would Abraham himself be blessed, but also he would be a blessing to others. In what specific ways and to whom is not defined here, but at the end of 12:3 this blessing shall be expanded and further defined.

5. *I will bless those who bless you.*

In addition to the blessings for Abraham and those whom he would be a blessing to, there was a special blessing from God for those who also blessed Abraham. Abraham would hold a special place in the heart of God, and be treated with unique esteem.

6. *The one who curses you I will curse.*

In contrast to the blessing for those who bless Abraham is a curse for those who curse him. This will become evident as nations are judged harshly for their treatment of the nation that Abraham fathered.

7. *In you all the families of the earth shall be blessed.*

This seventh promise affects not just those who bless or curse, but it will impact people from every nation. Again, no specifics are yet given, but it is evident that not only would Abraham be a blessing (the fourth promise) but through him the entire world would be blessed. It is in this seventh promise that God's earlier promise of redemption (Genesis 3:15) would be kept.

The Elements

1. *People*

Genesis 13:16 expands on this element:

> And I will make your descendants as the dust of the earth; so that if anyone can number the dust of the earth, then your descendants can also be numbered.

2. *Land*

Genesis 13:14-15 is more specific regarding this element:

> ...Now lift up your eyes and look from the place where you are, northward and southward and eastward and westward;

> for all the land which you see, I will give it to you and to your descendants forever.

Also Genesis 15:18:

> ...To your descendants I have given this land, from the river of Egypt as far as the great river, the river Euphrates...

The land element is further expanded in Deuteronomy 30.

3. *Kingdom*

Explanation of this element is not found with specificity until it is completely unfurled in the Davidic Covenant of 2 Samuel 7. From this point forward, every word of Scripture points forward to the *gradual*, *literal*, and *complete* fulfillment of each of the promises in this covenant.

Genesis 12:1-25:11
God Relates To Abraham

God initiated His relationship with Abraham by making a covenant with him. Genesis 12:1-25:11 contains the account of the rest of Abraham's life – an account that further illustrates God's character as the Covenant Keeper.

God tells Abraham to leave his home and follow God to a land that God would show him. Abraham was faithful in this, yet he shows his weakness in other areas. For example, in chapter 12 he does not trust God to protect him from the Egyptians, so he lies. In chapter sixteen, Abraham does not trust God to provide him with a son as promised. As a result he takes his wife's Egyptian maid as a concubine and she bears him a son, named Ishmael. God had promised to bless Abraham's descendants, and He indeed would bless Ishmael. Abraham's lack of trust would cause strife for thousands of years between the descendants of Ishmael and those of Isaac. In spite of Abraham's initial lack of trust, God kept His promise, and in Genesis 21 Isaac is born.

Even at this point, God was not finished teaching Abraham about faith. In Genesis 22 God tells Abraham to sacrifice Isaac as an offering to God. It is worth noting that never elsewhere in Scripture does God request physical human sacrifice (as was the practice of other pagan religions during Abraham's day). God was simply putting Abraham's faith to the test in terms he could understand, as well as providing a powerful illustration of His plan of salvation for man.

Even though he didn't yet know what God had in store, Abraham was faithful in this. As he was about to commit the act, the Angel of the Lord (the pre-incarnate Christ, Himself) stops him and shows him a ram in the thicket that would take Isaac's place. God provided an important picture of the work He would accomplish in order to bring fallen mankind back to Himself: He would give His only Son as a sacrifice. The ram in the thicket was a substitute for Isaac. Isaac was to die, but by the grace of God there was a substitute. As Scripture unfolds, it will soon become clear that Jesus Christ is the Substitute – the Redeemer who would pay for man's sin.

As Abraham's life comes to a close, he was "satisfied with life" (25:8), as the Lord had blessed him greatly. Even though he was not the perfect example of faith, he was an example nonetheless. Abraham began to understand that God would keep His promises, and even as he saw them begin to unfold in his lifetime (with the birth of Isaac, etc.), there was indeed much more to come. Through Abraham the promises of God can be traced, and the thread continues with Isaac.

Genesis 15:13-14
The Egyptian Exile and Exodus

As God ratifies His covenant with Abraham, He adds a bit of strange news:

> Know for certain that your descendants will be strangers in a land that is not theirs, where they will be enslaved and oppressed four hundred years. But I will also judge the

nation whom they serve; and afterward they will come out with many possessions (15:13-14).

Why, after promising to give Abraham's descendants the land would God pull them out again? He says in verse 16 that the "the iniquity of the Amorite is not yet complete." Amazingly, even amidst the wickedness of nations, God shows incredible patience. There was an allotted amount of sin that God would allow the Amorites to commit, and then it would be over. At the right time He would restore the descendants of Abraham to the land, thereby judging the Amorite. That promise is fulfilled in Egypt shortly after Joseph's time.

Genesis 15:18-21
The Land Covenant

God adds yet another measure of precision to His covenant with Abraham when He says,

> To your descendants I have given this land, from the river of Egypt as far as the great river, the river Euphrates: the Kenite and the Kenizzite and the Kadmonite and the Hittite and the Perizzite and the Rephaim and the Amorite and the Canaanite and the Girgashite and the Jebusite (15:18-21).

The Land Covenant unquestionably required a literal and physical fulfillment. The boundaries included in this promise are boundaries that Israel to this day has never attained. But God demonstrates patience and a methodical accomplishment of His plan to the extent of completion. His promise will not fail. The descendants of Abraham, through Isaac, will dwell in the land into eternity.

The specific nations mentioned become significant particularly when the nation of Israel begins her conquest of the land. How will Israel handle these nations? Will it be in accordance with the instruction of the Lord, or will she fall short? This is a key element of the history of Israel, and the question is answered in the latter part of Joshua and the early part of Judges.

Genesis 16:10-14
The Promise Regarding Ishmael

In God's covenant with Abraham, God promised to bless him and make a great nation from him. Abraham tried to assist God, becoming the father of Ishmael. This was a faithless act that would generate substantial conflict throughout the ages. We often recognize Abraham for his faith, but we must also not forget his faithlessness and the consequences it brought.

Because Ishmael was a son of Abraham, God promised to Hagar, Ishmael's mother, that He would bless Ishmael:

> I will greatly multiply your descendants so that they shall be too many to count...Behold you are with child, and you shall bear a son; and you shall call his name Ishmael, because the Lord has given heed to your affliction. And he will be a wild donkey of a man, his hand will be against everyone, and everyone's hand will be against him; and he will live to the east of his brothers (16:10-12).

Ishmael would be the father of a great nation, a nation of violence and strife. An epic ages-long struggle was about to begin.

Genesis 17:17-21
The Promise Regarding Isaac

Ishmael would be blessed by God, but he was not the son through whom God would carry out His Abrahamic Covenant:

> And I will bless her [Sarah], and indeed I will give you a son by her...and you shall call his name Isaac; and I will establish My covenant with him for an everlasting covenant for his descendants after him. And as for Ishmael, I have heard you; behold I will bless him, and will make him

> fruitful, and will multiply him exceedingly...But My covenant I will establish with Isaac... (17:16b, 19, 20-21a).

Abraham found the promise of a son born to him and Sarah in their old age difficult to fathom, yet God had made the promise, and He intended to keep it. The covenant would be established through Isaac, not Ishmael. As a result of Abraham's failure, there has been war between the descendants of Isaac and Ishmael ever since, and will be until the Abrahamic Covenant sees its final fulfillment.

Genesis 25
From Isaac to Jacob

Abraham's two sons, Isaac and Ishmael would play a vital role in world history. In chapter twenty-five we find that Ishmael did indeed become the father of a nation and that he brought strife early on. "He settled in defiance of all his relatives" (25:18). God's promise regarding Ishmael was fulfilled, but it was through Isaac that God would fulfill His covenant with Abraham. Isaac became the father of two sons, Esau and Jacob. They were born a very short time apart from each other, with Esau being the firstborn, and therefore having the rights of inheritance as the firstborn. But God had a different plan, as He told Rebekah:

> Two nations are in your womb; and two peoples shall be separated from your body; and one people shall be stronger than the other; and the older shall serve the younger (25:23).

Esau placed little value on his inheritance, as he willingly gave it away for some stew (25:25).

Isaac, like his father had a problem with trusting God. He acted in the same manner as Abraham, lying to protect himself in Egypt. This lack of trust notwithstanding, God still kept His promises through these men. As Isaac neared the end of his days he sought to bless his son Esau, for he loved him. It was through Esau that Isaac wished for God to keep His promises. But even in

Isaac's desire to bless Esau, the sovereignty of God is evident. God used Jacob's ambitious and deceptive spirit to place a dying father's blessing on Jacob. Isaac, try though he may, could not alter the will of God.

Once again, God had chosen a man to be chosen, and another He chose not to be chosen. God at first chose Isaac, and now He chooses Jacob. As the covenant promises become more specific, so too does the line through whom they would be kept. That the covenant promises would be kept through the line of Jacob becomes even more evident in the next promises God makes.

Genesis 28:10-17
God's Promise to Jacob

> ...I am the Lord, the God of your father Abraham and the God of Isaac; the land on which you lie, I will give it to you and your descendants. Your descendants shall also be like the dust of the earth, and you shall spread out to the west and to the east and to the north and to the south; and in you and in your descendants shall all the families of the earth be blessed. And behold, I am with you, and will keep you wherever you go, and will bring you back to this land; for I will not leave you until I have done what I have promised you (28:13-15).

Here the previous covenants are made more specific. It is now clear that the covenants run through Jacob. Here God reiterates the Land Covenant, as well as the seventh promise of the Abrahamic Covenant – that all families of the earth shall be blessed through Abraham's seed, and now, specifically through Jacob's.

Jacob was also granted a unique relationship with God to this point, even resulting in his name being changed to *Israel* (32:24-28). Israel would become father to twelve sons who would become the mighty nation named after their father. Through them, the promises would unfold further still.

Genesis 49:10
Judah: The Tribe of Royalty

"The scepter shall not depart from Judah..." (49:10). This is a vital promise that directs the future leadership of Israel through the tribe of Judah. Although it will be hundreds of years before this promise will begin to be fulfilled, God once again gives an insight into His plan, and we will see this promise ultimately fulfilled in Christ Jesus.

The Tribes of Israel
Reuben – the firstborn, son of Leah
Simeon – son of Leah
Levi – son of Leah, chosen to be a priestly tribe
Judah – son of Leah, chosen to be the tribe of Messiah, southern tribe
Dan – son of Bilhah (Rachel's maid), northernmost tribe
Naphtali – son of Bilhah
Gad – son of Zilpah (Leah's maid)
Asher – son of Zilpah
Issachar – son of Leah
Zebulun – son of Leah
Joseph – first son of Rachel, favored by Jacob
Benjamin – youngest son of Jacob, by Rachel, southern tribe
Manasseh – firstborn son of Joseph, a half tribe in place of Levi
Ephraim – youngest son of Joseph, blessed by Jacob, half tribe in place of Levi

JOB

J o b		1-2	Job's Testing
	Job's Dialogue	3	Job's Lamentation: Better to not have been born
		4-5	Eliphaz Speaks: Unrighteous deserve judgment
		6-7	Job's Response: Proclamation of innocence
		8	Bildad Speaks: God is just, therefore Job sinned
		9-10	Job's 2nd Response: God has not dealt justly
		11	Zophar Speaks: Assertion of Job's guilt
		12-14	Job's 3rd Response: Worthless physicians
		15	Eliphaz' 2nd Speech: Job, Detestable and Corrupt
		16-17	Job's 4th Response: Sorry comforters
		18	Bildad's 2nd Speech: Fate of the wicked
		19	Job's 5th Response: God has wronged me
		20	Zophar's 2nd Speech: Portion of the wicked
		21	Job's 6th Response: God's dealing with the wicked
		22	Eliphaz' 3rd Speech: Yield now to God
		23-24	Job's 7th Response: God's dealing with the wicked
		25	Bildad's 3rd Speech: Man cannot be just
	3-42:9	26-31	Job's 8th Response: I have been righteous
		32-37	Elihu Speaks: God is Righteous
		38-39	God's 1st Rebuke of Job
		40:1-5	Job Responds: Acknowledgment of insignificance
		40:6 – 41:34	God's 2nd Rebuke of Job
		42:1-6	Job Repents
		42:7-9	God Rebukes Eliphaz, Bildad, Zophar
	42:10-17		Job's Restoration

Authorship

Although the author is not identified within the book of Job, likely candidates include Job himself, or perhaps even Moses. The timeframe and setting of the book most likely fit into the patriarchal era of Genesis (in part due to the absence of any references to Israelite culture), and the book could have been written between the time of Moses and Ezra, although probably much earlier if authored by Job.

Documentary Or Drama?

Job's existence as a historical person is questioned by some, but Biblical authors refer to him as a historical figure:

> Ezek. xiv. 14 (cf. v. 16-20) speaks of 'Job' in conjunction with 'Noah' and 'Daniel', real persons. St. James (v.11) also refers to Job as an example of 'patience' which he would not have been likely to do had Job been only a fictitious person. Also, the names of persons and places are specified with such a particularity not to be looked for in an allegory.[5]

In addition to the internal evidence for the historicity of Job there is external linguistic evidence as well, specifically the use of the name *Iyyob* at such an early date. This was also the name of a Syrian prince in the eighteenth century BC. The book references the name Bildad, which was a shortened form of the name Yabil-Dadum, which was found in cuneiform writings during the same period.[6]

The book of Job is more than a divine play or a parable. Job is a historical example of God's sovereignty manifested in the lives of men. The question the book considers is *Why does God allow the righteous to suffer?* The solution is evident throughout, as man does not have the perspective and cognitive capability to grasp the entirety of God's dealings in any particular situation. He is sovereign and omnipotent. He will do as He will, in accordance with His plan, and humanity can only come to grips with that by recognizing our own lack of perspective and by acknowledging His perfect perspective.

The book of Job is the perfect prelude to the unfolding of God's promises, as many questions will surely arise in the minds of humanity in regard to the direction that God has taken or will take in human history. Without a doubt His thoughts are truly beyond human capability, but if we will simply wait upon Him and take Him at His word we will understand His glory, and we will grasp at least a fair degree of His purpose in history.

> 'For my thoughts are not your thoughts, neither are your ways my ways', declares the Lord. 'For as the heavens are higher than the earth, so are My ways higher than your ways, and my thoughts than your thoughts.' (Is. 55:8-9).

Purpose

God teaches us to rely on Him despite the *appearance* of circumstances. Job models that lesson when he says:

> Naked I came from my mother's womb, and naked I shall return there. The Lord gave and the Lord has taken away. Blessed be the name of the Lord (Job 1:21).

and

> I know that Thou canst do all things, and that no purpose of Thine can be thwarted. Who is this that hides counsel without knowledge? Therefore I have declared that which I did not understand, things too wonderful for me, which I did not know. Hear now and I will speak; I will ask Thee, and do Thou instruct me. I have heard of Thee by the hearing of the ear; but now my eye sees Thee; Therefore I retract, and I repent in dust and ashes (Job 42:2-6).

EXODUS   1525-1440 BC

Exodus: Israel From Slavery to Freedom	Out of Egypt: Israel Delivered From Slavery 1-15:22		1	Preparation of Israel for Deliverance
			2-4:28	Preparation of Moses
		Moses & Aaron Speak for God 4:29-12:30	4:29-10:29	First Nine Plagues
			11-12:28	Instructions Regarding Passover
			12:28-30	Tenth Plague
		12:31-15:22		Exodus of Israel: Deliverance
	Onward to Sinai: Israel Preserved 15:23-18:27	15:23-27		Rebellion and Provision: Water
		16		Rebellion and Provision: Manna
		17:1-7		Rebellion and Provision: Water
		17:8-16		Battle of Amalek: The Rise of Joshua
		18		Delegation of Authority
	At Sinai: Israel Prepared for the Journey 19-40	19		Preparation for the Law
		Giving Of The Law 20-31	20-24	General Laws
			25-31	Laws Regarding the Tabernacle
		32		Breaking of the Law
		33		Promise of Mercy
		34-35:19		Second Giving of the Law
		35:20-40:33		Obedience to the Law: Tabernacle Built
		40:34-38		The Glory of the Lord Fills the Tabernacle

Key Promises

Title

The Hebrew title, *w'ele sh'mot* is the first phrase, meaning *these are the names of...* The English is a transliteration of the Greek word *exodus*, meaning *a way out.*

Exodus 6:2-8; 12:12-13

The Exodus

In Genesis 15 God had told Abraham that there would be a four hundred year exile for Abraham's descendants. True to His word, the Israelites became slaves in Egypt for a period of about 400 years. But God had also said there would be an end to this enslavement:

> I am the Lord; and I appeared to Abraham, Isaac, and Jacob, as God Almighty, but by My name, Lord, I did not make Myself known to them. And I also established My covenant with them, to give them the land of Canaan, the land in which they had sojourned. And furthermore I have heard the groaning of the sons of Israel, because the Egyptians are holding them in bondage; and I have remembered My covenant. Say, therefore, to the sons of Israel, 'I am the Lord, and I will bring you out from under the burdens of the Egyptians, and I will deliver you from their bondage. I will also redeem you with an outstretched arm and with great judgments. Then I will take you for My people, and I will be your God; and you shall know that I am the Lord your God, who brought you out from under the burdens of the Egyptians. And I will bring you to the land which I swore to give to Abraham, Isaac, and Jacob, and I will give it to you for a possession; I am the Lord' (6:2-8).

God's deliverance of Israel would include Israel's departure with many possessions (Gen. 15), entry into Canaan (Ex. 6:4), and a unique relationship with God (Ex. 6:7). God's promise of a national deliverance was accompanied by a means for personal deliverance, prefiguring the work of Christ:

> For I will go through the land of Egypt on that night, and will strike down all the first-born in the land of Egypt, both men and beast; and against all the gods of Egypt I will execute judgments – I am the Lord. And the blood shall be a sign for you on the houses where you live; and when I see the blood I will pass over you, and no plague will befall you to destroy you when I strike the land of Egypt (12:12-13).

Here the theme of deliverance requiring blood is echoed. Previously we saw that Cain's sacrifice of the work of his hands was insufficient, whereby Abel's sacrifice – which required the shedding of blood – was acceptable to God (Gen. 4). Then we saw Isaac delivered by the substitutionary death of the ram (Gen. 22). The theme of substitutionary redemption by blood is an important illustration of what Christ would accomplish on the cross. He was the substitutionary Lamb Who would pay the penalty for sin.

After demonstrating His sovereignty through signs, plagues, and the hardening of Pharaoh's heart, God used Moses to lead Israel out from Egypt, and on toward the Promised Land.

Exodus 20
The Mosaic Covenant

Exodus 20 contains the Ten Commandments, and begins God's covenant with Israel through Moses. The whole of the Mosaic Covenant included 613 laws pertaining to every area of Israelite life. Perhaps no other covenant in Scripture has been so misunderstood and misapplied. It had a very specific purpose, and it had a very specific scope. It is later referred to as the Old Covenant (Jer. 31), because a New one was necessary to accomplish all that the old one could not. It must also be noted that what the Old Covenant was unable to accomplish, it was not *intended* to accomplish.

Characteristics of The Mosaic Covenant

National

The covenant was made specifically with Israel and with no other nation. It was also made with Israel as a whole, not with the individual. National obedience would result in national blessing. For example, consider this well known declaration:

> [if] My people who are called by My name humble themselves and pray and seek My face and turn from their wicked ways, then I will hear from heaven, will forgive their sin, and will heal their land (2 Chron. 7:14).

This promise of national restoration is followed by a lesser-known promise of national condemnation:

> But if you turn away and forsake My statutes and My commandments which I have set before you and shall go and serve other gods and worship them, then I will uproot you from My land which I have given you (2 Chron. 7:19-20a).

Note that punishment and reward deal with Israel's ability to remain in the land, not with individual salvation or justification. The Law (or Mosaic Covenant) was never intended or empowered to save.

Conditional

God's covenant with Israel through Moses was indeed a conditional covenant (Ex. 23:22). It promised blessing upon the nation if the nation remained obedient to the Law. The converse is thusly true: national disobedience would be a violation of this covenant, and therefore, since the covenant was ratified by both parties involved (God and Israel, Ex. 24:7-8), this same disobedience would invalidate the contract and make it null and void. In that case God would no longer be obligated by His word to bless the nation, but would then render judgment upon the nation, specifically to cast them out from the Promised Land (further detail on these conditions can be found in Lev. 26). This is the only significant conditional covenant that God made. The other key promises and covenants rested solely upon Him for their fulfillment.

Physical

The blessings and cursings of the covenant were decidedly physical. They dealt with God's grace in leading the Israelites into the land "flowing with milk and honey." Recall 2 Chronicles 7, which also made it evident that Israel's ability to dwell in the land was the key issue. It must then be noted that the Mosaic Covenant was not intended to address the Israelites' individual spiritual conditions.

Unattainable

The Mosaic Covenant never had the ability to bring redemption. Instead it was designed to make its constituents aware of their need for redemption. Therefore, built into this covenant was an intended inadequacy that would be compensated for, especially by the New Covenant. God built this covenant to serve a purpose, and once its purpose was complete it was thereby fulfilled. In hindsight it is evident that God's expectation was for Israel to fall short of keeping this covenant. An example of this sovereign intent is found in Deuteronomy 15:4-5, which states,

> However, there shall be no poor among you, since the Lord will surely bless you in the land which the Lord your God is giving you as an inheritance to possess, if only you listen obediently to the voice of the Lord your God, to observe carefully all this commandment which I am commanding you today.

It seems from this passage that Israel had the option of success, but an examination of 15:11, shows otherwise: "For the poor will never cease to be in the land..." God says again in Deuteronomy 30:11, "For this commandment which I command you today is not too difficult for you, nor is it out of reach..." God made it very clear what He required, understanding the Law would not be difficult to understand. Keeping it would be, however. Also, note Deuteronomy 30:1:

> So it shall be when all of these things have come upon you, the blessing and the curse which I have set before you, and you call them to mind in the nations where the Lord your God has banished you...

In prophetic voice Moses announces God's promise of restoration, but restoration could not be given unless judgment was first. God had given the Israelites a Law that they would be unable to keep, and their failure – even though they were held individually and nationally responsible – plays a key role in the fulfillment of God's other promises, the unconditional ones.

The Purpose of The Mosaic Covenant

Reading forward a bit in the Bible, we discover the purpose for the Law: "Therefore the Law has become our tutor to lead us to Christ, that we may be justified by faith" (Gal. 3:24). In short, the Law served to demonstrate that humanity in all our efforts could not attain to the holiness of God, and consequently we could not receive deliverance by the works of our hands. The Mosaic Covenant showed a degree of the true measure of the holiness of God, and Israel fell far short. Thus, the need for the substitutionary work of Christ becomes clear, and the vague redemptive reference of Genesis 3:15 is unveiled a bit further.

LEVITICUS

Leviticus: Laws of a Holy God	1-10 Concerning Holy Offerings	For People 1-6:7	1	Burnt Offering	
			2	Grain Offering	
			3	Peace Offering	
			4	Sin Offering	
			5-6:7	Guilt Offering	
		For Priests 6:8-10:20	6:8-13	Burnt Offering	
			6:14-23	Grain Offering / Priestly Offering	
			6:24-30	Sin Offering	
			7:1-10	Guilt Offering	
			7:11-34	Peace Offering	
			7:35-38	Explanation	
			8-9	Obedience: Aaron as Priest	
			10	Disobedience: Nadab and Abihu	
	11-22 Concerning Holy People	For People 11-15	11	Regarding Food	
			12	Regarding Reproduction	
			13-14	Regarding Disease (Leprosy)	
			15	Regarding Issue From Men and Women	
		16	For Priests:	Regarding the Holy Place	
		People & Priests 17	17:1-9	Regarding Location of Offerings	
			17:10-16	Regarding Blood	
		For People 18-20	18	Regarding Sexual Morality	
			19-20	General Laws	
		For Priests 21-22	21	Regarding Holy People	
			22	Regarding Holy Things	
		Concerning Holy Times 23-25	23:1-3	Regarding Sabbath	
			23:4-8	Regarding Passover	
			23:9-14	Regarding Firstfruits	
			23:15-22	Regarding Pentecost (50 days)	
			23:23-25	Regarding Trumpets	
			23:26-32	Regarding Day of Atonement	
			23:33-44	Regarding Tabernacles (Booths)	
			24	Regarding Lamps, Bread, Punishment	
			25	Regarding Jubilee, Sabbatical Year	
		26	The Picture of Holiness:	The Mosaic Covenant	
		27	The Value of Holiness:	Vows and Tithes	

Key Promise

The Exile From The Promised Land----------Lev. 25:1-4; 26:1-46

The Offerings of Mosaic Law						
What	Burnt	Grain	Peace	Sin	Guilt	Ordination
Why	Atonement for the Individual	Reminder of Provision, Gratitude	Remind of Fellowship With God Through Blood	Atonement For Sin of Person, Nation, Priest, or Leader	Atonement For Sin Against Holy Things (Days, Feasts, Tithes,etc.)	Ordination For Aaronic Priesthood
When	Anytime For Sin; Passover, First fruits, Pentecost, Trumpets, Day of Atonement Booths	Anytime: Gratitude, Commit, Passover, First fruits, Pentecost, Trumpets, Atonement Booths	Anytime For Thanks & To Commit	Anytime For Sin	Anytime For Sin	Consecration of Aaron and His Sons
How	From the Herd, From the Flock, Of Birds	Baked In An Oven, Made On Griddle, In Pan, Of early Ripened Things	Of the Herd, Of the Flock, A Goat	Bull, Goat, Turtledoves, Pigeons, Flour	A Ram	Various
Where	Leviticus 1,6,23 Numbers 28	Leviticus 2,6,23 Numbers 28	Lev. 3,7	Lev. 4,6,23 Num. 28	Leviticus 5,6,7	Exodus 28 Leviticus 6

Title

The Hebrew title is *w'yiq'ra*, meaning *and He called*, again the first word of the Hebrew text. The English is from the Greek *levitikos*, meaning *pertaining to the Levites*.

Summary

As a compliment to the book of Exodus, Leviticus provides a dramatic exposition of the Mosaic Covenant. Detailing hundreds of specific laws regarding offerings, moral issues, and calendar emphases, the book further speaks to not only the weighty requirements of the holiness of God, but it also contains many types and illustrations of coming fulfillments, always revolving around the central theme of the necessity of substitutionary atonement - a work that Christ Himself would later accomplish.

Leviticus 25:1-4; 26:1-46
The Exile from the Promised Land

A command of great significance is given in Leviticus 25:

> When you come into the land which I shall give you, then the land shall have a sabbath to the Lord. Six years you shall sow your field, and six years you shall prune your vineyard and gather its crop but during the seventh year the land shall have a sabbath rest, a sabbath to the Lord (Lev. 25:2-4).

This law dealt specifically with how Israel was to treat the land she had been given by God. It involved agricultural wisdom, as it would enable the land to be even more prosperous. It served as yet another reminder of the character of God – pointing back to His work of creation, and acknowledging Him as Sovereign over all. This command would be important in determining how God would judge Israel's failure to abide by the covenant.

The consequences for disobeying the Mosaic Covenant are found in great detail (and harshness) in Leviticus 26, and they included Israel being removed from the land, so that the land could enjoy the sabbath years that Israel would fail to keep while dwelling in the land.

You, however, I will scatter among the nations and will draw out a sword after you, as your land becomes desolate and your cities become waste. Then the land will enjoy its Sabbaths all the days of the desolation, while you are in your enemies' land; then the land will rest and enjoy its Sabbaths. All the days of its desolations it will observe the rest which it did not observe on your Sabbaths, while you were living on it. (Lev. 26:33-35)

and also,

For the land shall be abandoned by them, and shall make up for its Sabbaths while it is made desolate without them. They, meanwhile shall be making amends for their iniquity, because they rejected My ordinances and their soul abhorred My statutes. Yet in spite of this, when they are in the land of their enemies, I will not reject them, nor will I abhor them as to destroy them, breaking My covenant with them; for I am the Lord their God." (Lev. 26:43-44)

This is the promise of a seventy year exile, later identified specifically in Jeremiah 25:11 and Daniel 9:2. Notably, this would be "the exact number of years of Sabbaths in 490 years, the period from Saul to the Babylonian Captivity."[7] Keil and Deilitzsch calculate the numbers exactly, and their lengthy comment on the issue is very worthwhile:

The term of seventy years mentioned is not a so-called round number, but a chronologically exact prediction of the duration of Chaldean supremacy over Judah. So the number is understood in 2 Chron. 36:21,22; so too by the prophet Daniel, when, Dan. 9:2, in the first year of the Median king Darius, he took note of the seventy years which God, according to the prophecy of Jeremiah, would accomplish for the desolation of Jerusalem. The seventy years may be reckoned chronologically. From the 4th year of Jehoiakim, i.e. 606 BC, till the 1st year of the sole supremacy of Cyrus over Babylon, i.e., 536 BC, gives a period of 70 years. This number is arrived at by means of the dates given by profane authors as well as those of the historians of Scripture. Nebuchadnezzar reigned 43 years, his son Evil-Marodach 2 years, Neriglissor 4 years, Labrosoarchad (according to Berosus) 9 months and Naboned 17 years (43+2+4+17 years and 9 months are 66 years and 9 months). Add to this 1 year – that namely which elapsed between the time when Jerusalem was first taken by Nebuchadnezzar, and the death of Nabopolassar and Nebuchadnezzar's accession, - add further the 2 years of the reign of Darius the Mede... and we have 69 ¾ years. With this the Biblical accounts also agree. Of Jehoiakim's reign these give 7 years (from his 4th till his 11th year), for Jehoichin's 3 months, for the captivity of Jehoiachin in Babylon until the accession of Evil-Marodach 37 years (see 2 Kings 25:27, according to which Evil-Marodach, when he became king set Jehoiachin at liberty on the 27th day of the 12th months, in the 37th year after he had been carried away). Thus, till the beginning of Evil-Marodach's reign, we would have 44 years and 3 months to reckon, thence till the fall of Babylonian empire 23 years and 9 months and 2 years of Darius the Mede, i.e., in all 70 years complete.[8]

The precision with which God weaves His historical plan is truly amazing, and it is yet another reason for us to humble ourselves in light of His complete sovereignty. As for Israel, the nation would break the Mosaic Covenant, and would be subject to the awful consequences. But even amidst the wrath and judgment of God, He would be merciful, and would restore Israel back to the land after 70 years of exile (Lev. 26:44-45).

The Appointed Times of Leviticus 23-25

Name	Time	Description	Purpose
Sabbath	Friday 6:00pm-Saturday 6:00pm	Day of rest on which no work was to be done	1.Rest 2. Illustration of God as Creator
Passover	14th day of the first month (Abib or Nisan), at twilight	Four days of preparation preceded Passover, and it was the precursor to the Feast of Unleavened Bread	1. Illustration of God as Savior 2. Prefiguring of Christ
Feast of Unleavened Bread	15th day of the first month (Abib or Nisan), at twilight	Included a seven day convocation, the 1st and 7th were days of rest, and the days in between featured offerings by fire	Illustration of God as Deliverer (reminder of sudden deliverance of Israel from Egypt)
Firstfruits/ Harvest	The day after the Passover Sabbath	Included burnt & grain offerings established as a perpetual statute	1. Illustration of God as Provider 2. Thanked God in advance for blessing
Pentecost (50 days)	The day after the seventh Sabbath from Firstfruits	Included grain, burnt, & sin offerings, also a perpetual statute	1. Illustration of God as Provider 2. Thanked God for past blessing
Feast of Trumpets	On the first day of the seventh month	A day of rest and offerings by fire	1. Reminder of God as deliverer 2. Reminder to God of Israel (Numbers 10:10)
Day of Atonement	On the 10th day of the seventh month	A Sabbath of rest, a national humbling of Israel, including offerings by fire	Reminder of God as Atoner, Redeemer, Savior
Feast of Booths	On the 15th day of the seventh month	An eight day feast during which Israel would live in booths (tents), included an offering by fire, time of rest, and assembly	Reminder of God as Dwelling Place (Ps.90), and God's provision for Israel during and after the Exodus
Sabbatical Year	Every seventh year	A time for the land to rest. No sowing or pruning would take place during this year	1. Reminder of God as Creator 2. Maximized the productivity of the land
Jubilee	Every 50th year	Release of debts, property, and slaves. A year of Redemption	1. God as Judge 2. Brought refreshing, replenishing, and justice

NUMBERS 1440-1400 BC

Numbers: Bound For The Promised Land	1-10:10 First Numbering: Preparations For The Journey		First Numbering: Preparations For The Journey	1-4	The First Numbering	
				5-6	Laws of Purity & Sanctity of Israel	
				7-8:4	Numberings of Offerings	
				8:5-26	Laws of Purity & Sanctity of Levi	
				9:1-14	Laws of Passover	
			Trumpets 9:15-10:10	9:15-23	The Explanation	
				10:1-10	The Instruction	
	10:11-14:45 The Journey		1st Journey 10:11-11:34	10:11-36	The Journey	
				11:1-34	The Rebellion	
			2nd Journey 11:35-12:15	11:35	The Journey	
				12:1-15	The Rebellion	
			3rd Journey 12:16-14:45	12:16	The Journey	
				13:1-25	The Sending of Spies	
				13:26-33	The Report of The Spies	
				14:1-10	The Response of Israel: Rebellion	
				14:11-45	The Judgment of God: Israel Will Wander	
	15-19	Preparing For The Wandering		15	Holiness Demanded of Israel	
				16:1-40	Rebellion Against Priesthood: Korah, Dathan, Abiram	
				16:41-50	Rebellion Against Priesthood	
		Authority Of The Priesthood 17-19		17	Attested To: The Rod of Aaron	
				18	Explained	
				19	Enacted: The Ordinance of the Law	
	20-25	The Wandering		20	Sin At Meribah, Harshness of Edom, Death of Aaron	
				21	Defeat of Canaan, Rebellion of Israel, Provision,, Sihon & Og	
				22-24	Balaam & Balak	
				25	Idolatry of Israel, Zealotry of Phinehas	
	26-36	Preparations For Entering The Promised Land		26	The Second Numbering	
				27	Plea of Zelophehad, Judgment of Moses, Call of Joshua	
			Laws 28-30	28-29	Concerning Offerings	
				30	Concerning Vows	
				31	Defeat of Midian	
				32	Settling of Reuben and Gad	
				33:1-49	Summary of Journey: Egypt to the Jordan River	
				33:50-36:13	Final Instructions	

Key Promise

The Wilderness Exile -------------------------------------Num. 14:28-35

Summary

The Hebrew title is *b'mid'bar*, which means *in the wilderness*, taken from the first verse, and describing the central theme of the book. The Latin *arithmoi*, translated *numbers* in English refers to the two numberings of the people taken in the book. The first census took place as Israel prepared to enter the Promised Land. Due to three subsequent rebellions by Israel, God determined that Israel would wander in the wilderness for forty years until the rebellious generation had died. The second census was conducted after the forty-year wandering, as Israel once again prepared to enter the Promised Land.

Numbers 14:28-35
The Wilderness Exile

Israel had been prepared by God to enter the Promised Land, yet she rebelled against Him three times, warranting the following proclamation:

> Surely all the men who have seen My glory and My signs which I performed in Egypt and in the wilderness yet have put Me to the test these ten times and have not listened to My voice shall by no means see the land which I swore to their fathers, nor shall any of those who spurned Me see it (Num. 14:22-23).

And again, God expounds on His promise with specificity:

> 'As I live', says the Lord, 'just as you have spoken in My hearing, so I will surely do to you; your corpses shall fall in this wilderness, even all your numbered men, according to your complete number from twenty years and upward, who

have grumbled against Me. Surely you shall not come into the land in which I swore to settle you, except Caleb the son of Jephunneh and Joshua the son of Nun. Your children, however whom you said would become prey – I will bring them in, and they shall know the land which you have rejected. But as for you, your corpses shall fall in the wilderness. And your sons shall be shepherds for forty years in the wilderness, and they shall suffer for your unfaithfulness, until your corpses lie in the wilderness. According to the number of days which you spied out the land, forty days, for every day you shall bear your guilt a year, even forty years, and you shall know My opposition. I, the Lord, have spoken, surely this I will do to all this evil congregation who are gathered together against Me. In this wilderness they shall be destroyed, and there they shall die' (Num. 14:28-35).

God's character is demonstrated here rather vividly. He will not tolerate disobedience, and He will judge it deliberately. But even as He judges He shows His mercy, for rather than dismissing the entire nation, thereby breaking His promise, He only judges the current generation, and even in that He is merciful, as he shows mercy to Caleb and Joshua, the two men who remained faithful. Israel would wander for forty years (most of the timeframe of the book of Numbers), and then would return, poised to receive the land promise of God.

DEUTERONOMY

Deuteronomy: 2nd Giving of Mosaic Covenant	Prologue 1-3		1	Preparation to Enter The Promised Land
			2:1-15	Wilderness Exile
			2:16-3:29	Conquest Begun & Narrated
	4-11	Commandments	4-5	Call to Obedience: 10 Commandments
			6	Call to Fear God
			7	Call to Purity
			8	Call to Remembrance
			9	Call to Humility
			10	Call to Changed Hearts
			11	Call to Renewal
	Statutes & Judgments 12-27		12	Regarding Offerings
			13	Regarding Idolatry
			14	Regarding Personal Holiness
			15	Regarding Sabbath Year
			16:1-17	Regarding Passover, Weeks, Booths
			16:18-18:8	Regarding Judges, Justice, Kings & Levites
			18:9-22	Regarding Spiritism & Prophets
			19	Regarding Cities of Refuge, Boundaries, Witnesses
			20	Regarding Warfare
			21	Regarding Crime & Relationships
			22	Regarding Various & Marital Laws
			23	Regarding Countrymen & Foreigners
			24-25	Regarding Marital & Various Laws
			26	Regarding Firstfruits & Tithe
			27	Regarding Curses
	Epilogue 28-34		28-29	Covenant Consequences
			30	Covenant Restoration & Call to Obedience
			31	Commission of Joshua
			32-34	Song, Blessings, & Death of Moses

Key Promises

The Exile From the Promised Land ----Deut. 28-30 (9:4-6; 15:4-5,11)

The Land Covenant ---Deut. 30

Summary

This is the final of the five books of Moses, and is titled in Hebrew from *ele ha d'barim*, the first words of the text, meaning *these the words*. The English is from the Greek *deutero* (second) and *nomos* (law) and refers to the theme of the book, which is the second giving of the Law.

As a complementary book to Numbers, Deuteronomy summarizes briefly the failed initial preparations to enter the land of Canaan and the wilderness exile, and then picks up with Israel's preparations for their second effort to enter the Promised Land. At that point, Moses presents the Law in detail to Israel yet again to remind them of the seriousness of the Covenant into which they had entered. Moses emphasizes the three areas of the Covenant: the commandments (4-11), and the statutes and judgments (12-27). Concluding the reminder, Moses gave stern warnings regarding failure to abide by the Covenant, and profound prophecies regarding Israel's response.

Deuteronomy 28-30 (9:4-6; 15:4-5, 11)
The Exile from the Promised Land

Israel had a tendency to respond with pride to the special stature that they enjoyed, but God reminded them that His choosing of them was based on His sovereignty and not their own national righteousness:

> Do not say in your heart when the Lord your God has driven them out before you, 'Because of my righteousness the Lord has brought me in to possess this land,' but it is because of the wickedness of these nations that the Lord is dispossessing them before you...Know, then, it is not

because of your righteousness that the Lord your God is giving you this good land to possess, for you are a stubborn people (9:4,6).

God would drive out the nations before Israel, in spite of Israel's stubbornness. But yet, if Israel remained disobedient, His patience would end, and they would be judged. Deuteronomy 15:4, 5, and 11 illustrate the surety of this. The consequences of disobedience would be intense:

> But it shall come about, if you will not obey the Lord your God, to observe all His commandments and His statutes with which I charge you today, that all these curses shall come upon you and overtake you...The Lord will make the rain of your land powder and dust; from heaven it shall come down on you until you are destroyed...So all these curses shall come on you and pursue you and overtake you until you are destroyed, because you would not obey the Lord your God by keeping His commandments and His statutes which He commanded you. And they shall become a sign and a wonder on you and your descendants forever (28:15,24,45-46).

Coupled with Leviticus 25-26, it is evident that the consequence of disobedience would be a seventy-year exile from the Promised Land. Yet, even in light of the severity, the judgment would not completely destroy the nation, as a remnant would emerge.

> Then you shall be left few in number, whereas you were as the stars of heaven for multitude, because you did not obey the Lord your God (28:62).

Deuteronomy 30
The Land Covenant (Reiterated)

Genesis 15:18-21 records the land element of the Abrahamic covenant, and Deuteronomy 30 ties this element to future generations of a restored remnant:

> So it shall be when all of these things have come upon you, the blessing and the curse which I have set before you, and you call them to mind in all nations where the Lord your God has banished you, and you return to the Lord your God and obey Him with all your heart and soul according to all that I command you today, you and your sons, then the Lord your God will restore you from captivity, and have compassion on you, and will gather you again from all the peoples where the Lord your God has scattered you. If your outcasts are at the ends of the earth, from there the Lord your God will gather you, and from there He will bring you back. And the Lord your God will bring you into the land which your fathers possessed, and you shall possess it; and He will prosper you and multiply you more than your fathers. Moreover the Lord your God will circumcise your heart and the heart of your descendants, to love the Lord your God with all your heart and with all your soul, in order that you may live. And the Lord your God will inflict all these curses on your enemies and on those who hate you, who persecuted you. And you shall again obey the Lord, and observe all His commandments which I command you today. Then the Lord your God will prosper you abundantly in all the work of your hand, in the offspring of your body and in the offspring of your cattle and in the produce of your ground, for the Lord will again rejoice over you for good, just as He rejoiced over your fathers; if you obey the Lord your God to keep His commandments and His statutes which are written in this book of the law, if you turn to the Lord your God with all your heart and soul (30:1-10).

God promises both physical and spiritual restoration, reiterating elements of the Land Covenant. Israel would indeed return to the Promised Land. Key elements of this covenant include:

1. A broken Mosaic Covenant (30:1)
2. Restoration from the worldwide *diaspora*, or scattering (30:3-4)
3. Great blessing in the land (30:5)
4. Spiritual restoration (30:6)
5. Retribution upon Israel's enemies (30:7)
6. Renewed national obedience (30:8)
7. A change of attitude on God's part toward Israel (30:9)

Conclusion

Deuteronomy closes with the song of Moses (ch. 32), recounting the mighty and merciful works of God in dealing with Israel; and Moses' blessing of each tribe (ch. 33). The account of Moses' death in chapter 34 was possibly written by Joshua.

JOSHUA   1400-1370 BC

Joshua: The Incomplete Conquest of Canaan	1	The Leadership of Joshua	
	Central Conquest 2-10:15	2	Rahab: Faith & Reward
		3-4	Crossing Jordan
		5	Circumcision of Israel
		6	Conquest of Jericho
		7	Achan's Sin & Israel's defeat at Ai
		8	Conquest of Ai
		9	Gibeon Deceives Israel
		10:1-15	Israel Defends Gibeon
	10:16-43	Southern Conquest	
	11	Northern Conquest	
	12	List of Defeated Kings	
	Land Divided 13-21	East of Jordan	13 Reuben, Gad, Half Tribe of Manasseh
			14 Caleb
		At Gilgal	15 Judah
			16 Half Tribe of Ephraim
			17 Manasseh (Double Portion)
		At Shiloh	18 Benjamin
			19 Simeon, Zebulun, Issachar, Asher, Naphtali, Dan
			20 Cities of Refuge (6)
			21 Cities of the Levites (48)
	Prologue 22-24		22:1-9 Joshuua Addresses Reuben, Gad, Manasseh
			22:10-34 Struggle for Purity: The Misunderstood Altar
			23-24 Joshua's Farewell & Israel's Commitment

Key Promise

Failed Conquest --Josh. 23:11-13

Key Issue

Incomplete Conquest ----------------------------Josh. 15:63; 16:10; 17:13

Authorship

Joshua 24:26 presents Joshua as the primary author, a probability supported by Jewish tradition (i.e., the Talmud). This would place the date of composition right around 1370 BC. The ending (which recorded Joshua's death) perhaps could have been written by a later priest or scribe, such as Ezra.

Summary

God's plan to bring Israel into the Promised Land would be continued by His man of choice, Joshua. After a slow start to the conquest, Joshua would lead the nation of Israel on campaigns to the Central, Southern, and Northern parts of Canaan, and the tribes of Israel would receive their inheritance

The nation and her leader were told specifically by God to be thorough in driving out the sinful nations of Canaan:

> When you cross over the Jordan into the land of Canaan, then you shall drive out all the inhabitants of the land from before you, and destroy all their figured stones, and destroy all their molten images and demolish all their high places; and you shall take possession of the land and live in it, for I have given the land to you to possess it. And you shall inherit the land by lot according to your families; to the larger you shall give more inheritance and to the smaller you shall give less inheritance. Wherever the lot falls to anyone, that shall be his. You shall inherit according to the tribes of your fathers. But if you do not drive out the inhabitants of the land from before you, then it shall come about that those whom you let remain will become as pricks in your eyes and

as thorns in your sides, and they shall trouble you in the land in which you shall live. And it shall come about that as I plan to do to them, so I will do to you (Num. 33:51-56).

Joshua 15:63; 16:10; 17:13
Incomplete Conquest

Israel failed very quickly, as they allowed the Jebusites (15:63), and other Canaanites (16:10; 17:13) to remain – even using some as forced labor. The consequences would be severe.

Joshua 23:11-13
Failed Conquest

So take diligent heed to yourselves to love the Lord your God. For if you ever go back and cling to the rest of these nations, these which remain among you, and intermarry with them, so that you associate with them and they with you, know with certainty that the Lord your God will not continue to drive these nations out from before you; but they shall be a snare and a trap to you, and a whip on your sides and thorns in your eyes, until you perish from off this good land which the Lord your God has given you.

It would not take long for Israel to see the consequences for their failure to drive out the inhabitants of the land. In a matter of a few years, God's promise in this regard would be fulfilled.

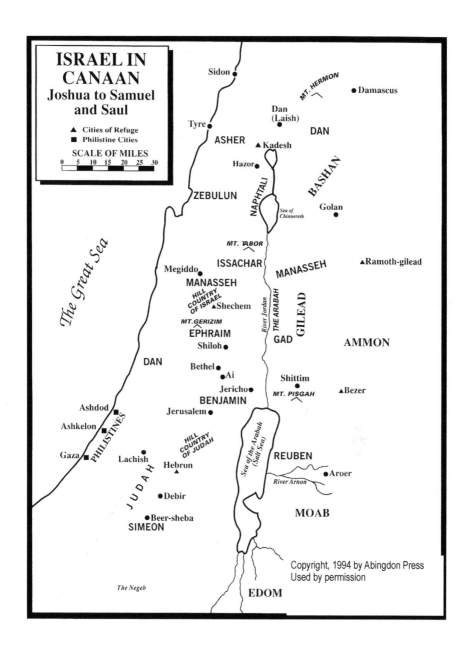

ISRAEL IN
CANAAN
Joshua to Samuel
and Saul

▲ Cities of Refuge
■ Philistine Cities

SCALE OF MILES
0   5   10   15   20   25   30

3

Promises Ignored

Theocracy Rejected

1370 - 1050 BC

Chronological Book

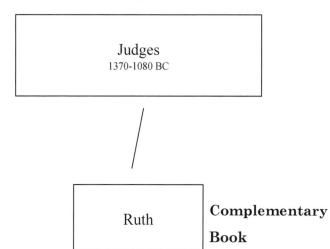

Judges
1370-1080 BC

Ruth

Complementary Book

Key Promise

The Mandate For Failed Conquest ---------- Judg. 1:27-2:23 (Ex. 23:31-33)

JUDGES   1370-1050 BC

Judges: Consequences of Incomplete Conquest	Conquest 1:1-3:8	1:1-26	Successful Conquest	
		1:27-3:8	Unsuccessful Conquest	
	The Judges 3:9-16:31	3:9-11	Othniel vs. Mesopotamia (Cushan-rishathaim)	40 years
		3:12-30	Ehud vs. Moab (Eglon) (+18 years before Ehud)	80 years
		3:31	Shamgar vs. Philistines	20 years
		4-5	Deborah & Barak vs. Canaan (Jabin & Sisera)	40 years
		6-8:32	Gideon vs. Midian	40 years
		8:33-9:57	Usurping of Abimelech	3 years
		10:1-2	Tola	23 years
		10:3-5	Jair	22 years
		10:6-12:7	Jephthah vs. Philistines & Ammonites	6 years
		12:8-10	Ibzan	7 years
		12:11-12	Elon	10 years
		12:13-15	Abdon	8 years
		13-16	Samson vs Philistines (+40 years before Samson)	20 years
	Conquest Vs. Impurity 17-21	17-18	Idolatry: Micah & The Tribe of Dan	
		19	The Evil of the Benjamites	
		20	Benjamin Defeated	
		21	Benjamin Preserved	

Key Promise

The Mandate For Failed Conquest -----------Judg. 1:27-2:23 (Ex. 23:31-33)

Background

Titled in Hebrew *shophetim,* and Greek *kritai,* both are translated *judges.* The Talmud attributes the authorship to Samuel, although this conclusion is not a certainty. The book covers a period of more than three hundred and twenty years.

Summary

Exodus 23:31-33 records God's mandate that Israel should be thorough in their conquest of the Canaanite nations:

> And I will fix your boundary from the Red Sea to the sea of the Philistines, and from the wilderness to the River Euphrates; for I will deliver the inhabitants of the land into your hand, and you will drive them out before you. You shall make no covenant with them or with their gods. They shall not live in your land, lest they make you sin against Me; if you serve their gods, it will surely be a snare to you.

Unfortunately, Israel failed decisively to obey the command. Judges 1:27-36 lists Israel's failings in this regard. The result was a cycle that continued for over 300 years.

Israel's failure was twofold: first, they did not completely drive out the nations as they were commanded. Second, just as they were warned, they became involved in idolatry with the nations they allowed to remain, and broke the Mosaic Covenant. As a result, God made it clear that He would not allow further progress for Israel:

> ...'Because this nation has transgressed My covenant which I commanded their fathers, and has not listened to My voice, I also will no longer drive out before them any of the nations which Joshua left when he died, in order to test Israel by them, whether they will keep the way of the Lord to walk in it as their fathers did, or not.' So the Lord allowed those nations to remain, not driving them out quickly; and He did not give them into the hand of Joshua (Judg. 2:21-23).

The cycle of defeat would continue throughout the times of the Judges and even into the Monarchy Period.

RUTH

1:1-5 Naomi's Loss	1:6-22 Ruth's Loyalty	2:1-7 Ruth's Diligence	2:8-23 Boaz' Kindness	3 Naomi's Plan: God's Provision	4:1-12 Boaz' Commitment	4:13-17 Obed's Birth	4:18-22 David's Lineage

Ruth: God Protects A Lineage

Key Issues

Lineage of David: Identified and Preserved

Kinsman Redeemer: Portrait of Christ

Background

Named after the primary character, the events of Ruth take place during the time of the Judges, and possibly during the time of Gideon. The events of Ruth occur during a national famine (Ruth 1:1), possibly due to Midianite oppression of a sort that was particularly painful for the produce of the land (Judg. 6:3-4). Such a famine prompted God's call of Gideon. The book of Ruth was not written until the time of David (note that the tracing of David's lineage is a key in the book). Samuel is generally considered to be the author, though we cannot be certain of the authorship.

Summary

The significance of the narrative can be seen particularly in the advancing and preserving of God's promise regarding the tribe of Judah (Gen. 49:10). God's revelation of promises becomes more specific as time goes on, and the narrative of Ruth underscores the lineage that will ultimately bring about Messiah.

Lineage of David: Identified and Preserved

Both Genealogies of Christ (Matthew's and Luke's) identify Boaz in the line of Messiah, of the tribe of Judah. He was without a wife, and thus childless, at the outset of the narrative. But as the historical account progresses, God uniquely provides a family for Boaz, and the lineage of fulfillment for the Abrahamic promises becomes apparent, although it is not until 2 Samuel 7 that we understand the true significance of the events of the book of Ruth.

Ruth is also identified by name in Matthew's genealogy of Christ (Mt. 1:5), which presents to some a quandary in light of the Moabite curse of Deuteronomy 23:3. However, there is no difficulty in consistency here, as the curse referred specifically to the masculine, while Ruth is precisely identified in the feminine (Ruth 1:22). It is also notable that she was daughter in law to Naomi, wife of Elimelech, of the tribe of Judah, and of Bethlehem. Her identification in the Gospel genealogy is significant, as Hebrew genealogies typically did not identify women. Her mention by name is perhaps due to her faith in the God of Israel, demonstrated in her loyalty and diligence.

Boaz and Ruth are blessed with a child – Obed, who would become the grandfather of David, the next Covenant son of promise.

Kinsman Redeemer: Portrait of Christ

While it is probably not appropriate to see Boaz as a *type* of Christ (since Scripture does not refer to him as such), Boaz demonstrates the Old Testament concept of redemption, serving as a portrait for the later accomplished work of Christ. Deuteronomy 25:5-10 describes the custom of Levirite marriage, whereby if a brother died childless, his brother would redeem the wife of the dead brother in order to give him an enduring posterity. Boaz carries out this duty for Ruth, and in so doing demonstrates a love and commitment of the same kind as that which is later shown in the redemptive work of Christ.

4

Promises Expanded

Monarchy

1050-586 BC

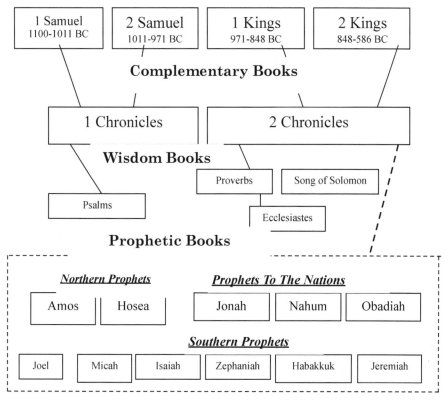

Chronological Books

1 Samuel	2 Samuel	1 Kings	2 Kings
1100-1011 BC	1011-971 BC	971-848 BC	848-586 BC

Complementary Books

1 Chronicles   2 Chronicles

Wisdom Books

Proverbs   Song of Solomon

Psalms   Ecclesiastes

Prophetic Books

Northern Prophets   *Prophets To The Nations*

Amos   Hosea   Jonah   Nahum   Obadiah

Southern Prophets

Joel   Micah   Isaiah   Zephaniah   Habakkuk   Jeremiah

Key Promises

The Davidic Covenant---2 Sam.7:8-17 (Jer. 33, Is. 60-66)

To Solomon---1 Kin. 9:1-9, 2 Chron. 7:11-22

The Day of the Lord---Joel 1:15; 2:2, 30-3:3

The Holy Spirit Promised ---Joel 2:28

Rulers of the Monarchy Period and Corresponding Books

					Historical Books	
1040 BC	*Wisdom Books*	Saul				
	Psalms, Proverbs				1 and 2	1 Chron.
1000	Ecclesiastes	David			Samuel	
	Song of Solomon					
		Solomon			1	
950					K	
	Southern Kingdom:				i	
	Judah		**Northern Kingdom:**		n	
			Israel		g	
					s	
	Rehaboam		**Jeroboam**			2
	Abijah		**Nadab**			
	Asa		**Baasha**			C
			Elahzimel			h
	Jehoshaphat	*Prophets*	**Tibni & Omri**			r
900	**Jehoram**		**Ahab & Ahaziah**			o
	Ahaziah	Obadiah }	**Joram**			n
850	**Athaliah**		**Jehu**		2	i
	Joash	{ Joel	**Jehoaz**			c
	Amaziah		**Jehoash**			l
	Uzziah	Amos }Jonah	**Jeroboam II**		K	e
		Hosea }	**Zechariah**		i	s
800	**Jotham**		**Shallum & Menahem**		n	
		{ Micah	**Pekahiah & Pekah**		g	
	Ahaz	{ Isaiah	**Hoshea**		s	
750	**Hezekiah**	{ Zephaniah				
	Manasseh	Nahum				
	Amon	{ Habakkuk				
	Josiah					
700	**Jehoahaz**					
	Jehoiakim	{ Jeremiah				
650	**Jehoiachin**					
	Zedekiah					

1 SAMUEL

1100-1011 BC

1 Samuel: Transition to Monarchy	The Period of Judges Concludes	1-8:3	1:1-2:10	The Birth of Samuel
			2:11-36	Samuel and Eli's Sons
			3	Call of Samuel
			4-6	The Philistines & the Ark
			7:1-14	God Delivers Israel: Philistine Defeat
			7:15-17	Samuel: Faithful Judge
			8:1-3	Samuel's Sons: Unfaithful Judges
	The Monarchy Begins: Saul as King	8:4-31:13	8:4-22	Israel Seeks a King
			9	Saul Chosen as King
			10	Saul Confirmed as King
			11	Saul Victorious as King
			12	Samuel's Address & Israel's Repentance
			13:1-10	Saul Wars as King (vs. Philistines)
			13:11-23	Saul Acts as Priest
			14:1-46	Saul's Foolishness & Jonathan's Bravery
			14:47-52	Saul's Conquest
			15	Failure & Judgment of Saul
			16	Rejection of Saul: David Anointed
			17	David Confirmed: Defeat of Goliath
			18	David Loved: Jonathan & Michal
			19	David Protected: Saul's Hatred
			20	David Protected: Jonathan's Loyalty
			21	David Provided For: Ahimalech the Priest
			22	Saul's Hatred: Murder of the Priests
			23:1-14	David Victorious: At Keilah
			23:15-29	David Hated: Pursued by Saul
			24	David Merciful: Saul Spared
			25:1	The Death of Samuel
			25:2-44	The Strength of Abigail
			26	David Merciful: Saul Spared
			27	David Afraid: Escapes From Saul
			28	The Wickedness of Saul: Spiritism
			29	David Suspected: By the Philistines
			30	David Victorious (vs. Amalekites)
			31	Deaths of Saul & Jonathan

Authorship

In the Hebrew canon, 1 and 2 Samuel were considered to be one book, and were traditionally recognized as being authored by Samuel (1 Sam. 1-24), Nathan the prophet, and Gad the seer (1 Sam. 25ff). The books were probably completed around 975 BC.

Summary

Samuel served as both prophet (3:20) and judge (7:15), bridging the gap from the time of judges to the Monarchy Period. He presided over a nation who ultimately chose to be like the nations and have a human king (8:5) rather than submit to the leadership of God Himself. Even though God had promised Abraham a nation of descendants, it had not yet been revealed who would rule the nation. God would use Israel's desire for a human king as a vehicle for ultimately providing the nation with a Divine King. Nevertheless, Israel sought human leadership, manifesting their lack of faith (recall Israel's worship of the golden calves while Moses was still on the mountain). They demanded tangible evidences of God's blessing on the nation. This characteristic would be evident in Israel even during the time of Jesus' earthly ministry.

1 Samuel records the anointing and coronation of Israel's first human king, Saul of Benjamin. But Saul's failure to obey God (by assuming the priestly office, and his disobedience at Amalek, ch.13 and 15) resulted in God's rejection of Saul. God chose an unlikely candidate, David son of Jessie, of the tribe of Judah, to replace Saul. God's choosing of David was further confirmed by David's victory over Goliath (ch. 17), and by God's protection of David from an angry and jealous King Saul. The book closes with the judgment of Saul for his unfaithfulness, and his death at the hands of the Philistines. As a prelude to 2 Samuel, 1 Samuel narrows the focus to God's chosen man, David, who would be the benefactor of another grand promise of God, the Davidic Covenant (2 Sam. 7). This covenant would further reveal God's magnificent plan as His Abrahamic promises continued to unfold.

2 SAMUEL   1011-971 BC

2 Samuel: David - The Covenant King	Kingdom Divided 1-4:12	1	David Mourns Saul & Jonathan
		2:1-7	David Anointed King of Judah
		2:8-11	Ish-Bosheth King of Israel
		2:12-4:12	Civil War: House of Saul vs. House of David
	Kingdom United 5-14	5:1-5	David Anointed King of Israel
		5:6-25	David's Victories
		6	The Ark Brought to Jerusalem
		7	The Davidic Covenant
		8-10	David's Victories & Kindness to Mephibosheth
		11-12:23	David's Failures: Adultery & Murder
		12:24-25	Birth of Solomon
		12:26-31	David's Victories
		13-14	David's Failure: Family Strife
	Kingdom Endangered 15-20	15-19:7	Absalom's Failed Coup
		19:8-43	David's Reparations
		20	Sheba's Failed Coup
	Kingdom Protected 21-24	21	Gibeonites Receive Justice
		22-23:7	David's Psalm & Last Words
		23:8-39	David's Mighty Men
		24	David's Sinful Census & Repentance

Key Promises

The Davidic Covenant ----------------------------------2 Sam. 7:8-17

Summary

After the death of Saul, David is appointed king over the southern tribe of Judah. Saul's surviving son, Ish-Bosheth, was presented by Abner, the commander of Saul's army as the king of the rest of Israel. After a civil war and the murder of Ish-Bosheth by two of his own commanders, David became king over the entire nation. In a key conquest of the Jebusites, David captured the city of Jerusalem and established it as the new geographical focal point of Israel. He brought the Ark of the Covenant to Jerusalem and there planned to build a temple for the Lord.

2 Samuel 7:8-17

The Davidic Covenant

In response to David's desire to build the temple, God made a very important promise to David, and one that would further clarify God's intentions and methodology for keeping the Abrahamic Covenant. The Davidic Covenant contains seven key elements:

1. *I will make you a great name (7:9).*

Reminiscent of God's promise to Abraham, David is assured of the greatness of his name. Not only would he be renowned in his own generation, but also into eternity.

2. *I will also appoint a place for My people Israel and will plant them that they may live in their own place and not be disturbed again... (7:10).*

This was actually an odd promise in light of Israel's present circumstance. The nation was firmly entrenched in the Promised Land (although they had not yet attained to the borders promised in Gen. 15), and they were beginning a sort of golden age. God's promises to appoint a place and to plant them indicate that they would at some point be taken from the land. Of course that happened with the Exile, but this element includes also the promise that they would not be disturbed again. There would be a national, eternal peace. Israel still awaits this, and as further promises unfold, it becomes evident that the Millennial Kingdom of Christ will begin this peace.

3. *I will give you rest from all your enemies (7:11).*

While David did experience some years of peace, his early reign was characterized by war and conquest, while his latter reign was filled with family strife – even to the extent of war. The rest and peace David was unable to obtain during his reign would later be provided on a grand scale.

4. *The Lord will make a house for you (7:11).*

The previous promises necessitated this one. God would provide David an enduring lineage through which these promises would be kept, and through which the promises would gain ultimate fulfillment in Christ.

5. *I will raise up your descendant after you, who will come forth from you, and I will establish his kingdom (7:12).*

With this specific reference to Solomon, God again makes clear that His covenant will be kept through a particular line. The future establishment of the kingdom of Israel would take place through this descendant of David. Some suggest that this element has a near and far aspect (that it could be referring both to Solomon and ultimately to Christ), but this is neither likely (due to the references of committing iniquity in v.14) nor necessary (due to the specific language of the next element in v. 13).

6. *He shall build a house for My name, and I will establish the throne of his kingdom forever (7:13).*

Solomon would build a glorious temple. David here receives consolation, as he wished to build this temple but was forbidden (1 Chron. 28). Still he was assured that his own son would build it. This second aspect of this promise is very significant. God promises that He would "establish the throne of his kingdom forever." Note that it is not the kingdom that is established forever, rather it is the throne that would be established. There would be One from the line of Solomon, of the line of David, who would rule on this throne into eternity. David understood the significance of this, as he presents in Psalm 110 his praise to the King who was to come.

7. *Your throne shall be established forever (7:16).*

Consequently, the throne of David's kingdom would be established as well. Note that none of these promises are conditional. The responsibility for their fulfillment was with God and His sovereign working to complete them. They are all precise, and they all would come to pass in a very literal sense. Even though the latter part of David's rule was marred by revolts, wars, and family strife, He recognized that the Messiah King would come. In so doing he acknowledged that God would keep His promises.

1 CHRONICLES

1 Chronicles: The Reign of David	**1 Chronicles: The Reign of David**	1	Genealogy & Descendants of Abraham
		2	Descendants of Jacob
	Genealogies & Numberings	3	Descendants of David
		4:1-23	Descendants of Judah
		4:24-43	Descendants of Simeon
		5	Descendants of Reuben
		6	Descendants of Levi
		7	Of Issachar, Benjamin, Manasseh, Ephraim, Asher
		8	Descendants of Benjamin
		9:1-34	People of Jerusalem
	1-10	9:35-44	Genealogy & Descendants of Saul
		10	Death of Saul
	The Reign Of David	11-12	David's Kingdom: Anointing, Location, & Support
		13	The Ark Transported: Obed-Edom
		14	David's Kingdom Grows
		15	The Ark Transported: Jerusalem
		16	Celebration of the Ark
		17	Davidic Covenant
		18-20	David's Conquests
	11-21	21	David's Sinful Census
	Preparations For The Temple	22	Solomon Charged to Build the Temple
		23-24	Divisions of Levites
		25	Divisions of Musicians
		26	Divisions of Other Officials
		27	Divisions of Commanders, Officers, & Overseers
		28-29:22	David's Preparations for the Temple
	22-29	29:23-30	Solomon's 2nd Coronation & David's Death

Background

Titled *davari hayami'im* in Hebrew, meaning *events or words of the days*, the books of 1 and 2 Chronicles were united as one in the Hebrew canon as part of the Hagiographa – the ketuvi'im. The translator Hieronymus (of the Latin Vulgate) first attributed the title *Chronicles* to the books.

Ezra is traditionally regarded as the author, although it is evident that he utilized numerous sources in compiling the book (e.g., 1 Chron. 29:29; 2 Chron. 9:29, 12:15, 16:15, 20:34, 25:26, 33:19). Due to the priestly authorship (Ezra being both priest and scribe) the Chronicles focus on the primary issues of the reign of David (advancing the covenant promises), the temple preparations, and the spiritual condition of the nation. This is a notable contrast to the books of Kings, which focus on the historical exploits of the rulers and the prophets. 1 Chronicles parallels the timeframe of the latter parts of 1 Samuel and the entirety of 2 Samuel, while 2 Chronicles parallels the timeframe of 1 and 2 Kings. The Chronicles were probably completed approximately 450 BC.

Summary

The first section of the book deals with genealogies and lineages, primarily introducing the reign of David, and briefly demonstrating how Israel arrived at that stage of the nations history. Chapter seventeen recounts the Davidic Covenant, and with that, the focus of the book shifts to the preparations for building the temple, including the numbers and divisions of all ministry officers. The book concludes with David's blessing and prayer for the soon to be built temple, and for his successor - his Covenant son, Solomon.

1 KINGS   971-853 BC

1 Kings: Solomon and The Divided Kingdom	The Kingdom United: The Rule of Solomon 1-11	1	Solomon Becomes King	
		2:1-12	David's Charge to Solomon & His Death	
		2:13-46	Solomon's Kingdom Established	
		3	Solomon Given Wisdom	
		4	Solomon's Government	
		5-6	Solomon Builds the Temple	
		7:1-12	Solomon Builds His House	
		7:13-8:66	The Temple Completed & Dedicated	
		9:1-9	God's Promise to Solomon	
		9:10-10:13	Solomon's Foreign Dealings: Hiram & Queen of Sheba	
		10:14-29	Solomon's Greatness	
		11	Solomon's Failure & Death	
	The Kingdom Divided 12-22	12:1-25	Rehoboam over Judah, Jeroboam over Israel	
		12:26-14:20	Jeroboam's Sin, Judgment, & Death	
		14:21-31	Rehoboam's Sin & Death	
		15:1-8	Abijam King of Judah	(evil)
		15:9-24	Asa King of Judah	(righteous)
		15:25-31	Nadab King of Israel	(evil)
		15:32-16:28	Baasha, Elah, Zimri, Omri: Over Israel	(evil)
		16:29-34	Ahab King of Israel	(evil)
		17-19	Ministry of Elijah	
		20-21	Ahab's Conquests	
		22:1-40	Ahab's Defeat & Death	
		22:41-50	Jehoshaphat King of Judah	(righteous)
		22:51-53	Ahaziah King of Israel	(evil)

Key Promises

To Solomon: Established Throne ------------------------1 Kin. 9:1-9

Background

Like Samuel and Chronicles, 1 and 2 Kings are one book in the Hebrew canon but were divided later by the Alexandrian translators. Titled *meleki'im*, meaning *kings*, the books deal with the monarchy history of Israel, focusing on the kings and prophets, and how Israel journeyed from rich theocracy to enslaved exile. The authorship of Kings, while not known for certain, has been attributed by Jewish tradition to Jeremiah.

> Jewish tradition credited both 1 and 2 Kings to the prophet Jeremiah (Baba Bathra 15a), and there is much evidence to commend that view. First, Jeremiah lived about the time the book was completed. Second, if Jeremiah were the author, that might explain why the book considers the prophets to be almost as important as the kings. It might also explain how, for example, the author obtained information about Elijah and Elisha. Third, the author's general outlook reminds one of Jeremiah. That is, both this author and Jeremiah understood that idolatry was the main affliction of God's people.[9]

The author utilized several sources (see 1 Kin. 11:41, 14:19, 29) in compiling the book(s), and probably completed the book(s) around 550 BC.

Summary

The first eleven chapters deal with the final period of the United Kingdom of Israel: Solomon's reign as king. It was during this period that Israel enjoyed her greatest glory to date, as evidenced by the completing of Solomon's magnificent temple and the time of peace that immediately prefaced and followed. God reiterated elements of the Davidic Covenant to Solomon (9:1-9). Notably, like David's, the throne of Solomon's kingdom would be established forever. However, in 9:5 the statement "You shall not lack a man on the throne of Israel" lacks the word *forever*, which was present in the previous promise of an eternal throne. God explained that Israel would be cut off due to idolatry, and the kingdom would be broken temporarily until (as we see later) Israel's Messiah King from the line of David (and Solomon, see the genealogy of Christ in Mt. 1:6) would come to restore it. Just as God had promised, idolatry crept in even during Solomon's reign, and God began to rip away the Mosaic Covenant blessings of peace and prosperity.

The Divided Kingdom began in 931 BC, following Solomon's reign. This division is traced in 1 Kings from the reigns of Rehoboam in the South and Jeroboam in the North, to Jehoshaphat in the South and Ahaziah in the North. It is notable that during this time the Southern Kingdom of Judah only had two righteous kings, Asa and Jehoshaphat, while the Northern Kingdom of Israel had none – they were all evil. Even despite the ministry of Elijah during this period, Israel's violation of the Mosaic Covenant was nearing its breaking point. Judgment was coming.

THE
KINGDOMS
OF ISRAEL
AND JUDAH

SCALE OF MILES
0   10   20   30   40

Copyright, 1994 by Abingdon Press
Used by permission

Sidon
Damascus

PHOENICIA

KINGDOM OF
DAMASCUS

Tyre   Dan

ISRAEL

SAMARIA

River Jordan

The
Great
Sea

Joppa

Bethel

AMMON

JERUSALEM
Tokea
Moresheth

Gaza

PHILISTIA

Lake Asphaltitis
(Dead Sea)

JUDAH

Beersheba

MOAB

Kadesh-
barnea

EDOM

Arabian Desert

KINGDOM OF
EGYPT

Elath

N
W   E
S

2 KINGS   848-586 BC

2 Kings: The Monarchy Fails	The Divided Kingdom	1	Death of Ahaziah	
		2	Elisha Succeeds Elijah	
		3	Jehoram King of Israel	(evil)
		4-8:15	The Ministry of Elisha	
		8:16-24	Joram King of Judah	(evil)
		8:25-29	Ahaziah King of Judah	(evil)
		9-10	Jehu King of Israel	
		11:1-20	Athaliah Queen of Judah	(evil)
		11:21-12:21	Joash King of Judah	(good)
		13:1-9	Jehoahaz King of Israel	(evil)
		13:10-13	Jehoash King of Israel	(evil)
		13:14-21	Death of Elisha	
		13:22-25	God's Compassion: Victories of Jehoash	
		14:1-22	Amaziah King of Judah	(good)
		14:23-29	Jeroboam King of Israel	(evil)
		15:1-7	Azariah King of Judah	(righteous)
		15:8-12	Zechariah King of Israel	(evil)
		15:13-31	Shallum, Menahim, Pekahiah, & Pekah: of Israel (evil)	
		15:32-38	Jotham King of Judah	(good)
		16	Ahaz King of Judah	(evil)
		17:1-5	Hoshea King of Israel	(evil)
	1-17	17:6-41	The Northern Kingdom Falls To Assyria	
	The Remaining Kingdom: Judah	18-20	Hezekiah King of Judah	(righteous)
		21:1-18	Manasseh King of Judah	(evil)
		21:19-26	Amon King of Judah	(evil)
		22-23:30	Josiah King of Judah	(righteous)
		23:31-35	Jehoahaz King of Judah	(evil)
		23:26-24:6	Jehoiakim King of Judah	(evil)
		24:7-24:9	Jehoiachin King of Judah	(evil)
		24:10-16	Babylonian Exile	
		24:17-25:7	Zedekiah King of Judah	(evil)
		25:8-21	Babylonian Exile	
	18-25	25:22-26	Gedaliah Governor of Judah	
		25:27-30	Jehoiachin Honored	

Summary

Beginning with the death of Ahaziah, 2 Kings continues the Monarchy narrative. Not only did the early narrative cover transition in the rulership of Israel, but also there was significant change in the prophetic leadership of the day. Elisha succeeded Elijah, whom God took home in the chariot of fire (2:11). The history of the Divided Kingdom continues with the Northern Kingdom being ruled entirely by evil kings, while the Southern Kingdom did not fare much better. In the case of both the Northern and Southern Kingdoms, their judgment and fall are recorded in 2 Kings.

The first seventeen chapters conclude with the fall of the Northern Kingdom in 721 BC at the hands of the Assyrians. In addition to exiling the peoples of the North, Shalmanezer (and/or Sargon) brought in Assyrian peoples to inhabit the area of Samaria. These Assyrians intermarried with the Jews who remained in the area, as not all of the northern Jews were exiled. The progeny of these mixed marriages became known as Samaritans, and they were not highly regarded by the Jews during the intertestamental and early New Testament period, because the Samaritans were not perceived to be pure-blooded Israelites.

The final chapters of the book recount the last kings of Judah and the sieges of Jerusalem by Nebuchadnezzar king of Babylon, who in 605 BC became the dominant world power by defeating Egypt and Assyria (at the Battle of Carchemish). Nebuchadnezzar's first conquest of Judah came in 605 BC, during the reign of Jehoiakim (24:1-16). Judah became a slave nation until the rebellion of Zedekiah in 597 BC (24:17-25:10), upon which time Nebuchadnezzar arrived again, this time bringing crippling destruction on the still yet surviving city of Jerusalem – including the burning of the temple and all the great houses of Jerusalem. Finally in 586 BC, Nebuchadnezzar attacked a third time, deporting most of the remaining inhabitants. The exile began, just as God had promised. Israel had violated the Mosaic Covenant, and God brought judgment just as He had warned. But from those exiled would return a remnant who would represent the beginning of restoration for the nation.

2 CHRONICLES

2 Chronicles: Solomon & The Kings of Judah	The Reign of Solomon	1	Solomon Blessed
		2	Solomon's Preparation for the Temple
		3-5:1	Solomon Builds the Temple
		5:2-14	The Ark & The Glory of God in the Temple
	1-9	6-7:10	Solomon Dedicates the Temple
		7:11-22	God's Promise to Solomon
		8-9	The Greatness of Solomon
	The Divided Kingdom: The Kings of Judah	10-12	Rehoboam
		13	Abijah
		14-16	Asa
		17-20	Jehoshaphat
		21	Jehoram
		22	Ahaziah & Athaliah
		23-24	Joash
		25	Amaziah
		26	Uzziah
		27	Jotham
		28	Ahaz
		29-32	Hezekiah
		33:1-20	Manasseh
	10-36	33:21-25	Amon
		34-35	Josiah
		36:1-9	Joahaz, Eliakim (Jehoiakim), & Jehoiachin
		36:10	Zedekiah, Exile, & Return

Key Promises

To Solomon: Established Throne ------------------2 Chron. 7:11-22

Summary

Complementing the historical narrative of 1 and 2 Kings, 2 Chronicles concentrates its first nine chapters on the United Kingdom of Israel under the reign of Solomon. Highlighting this section is the account of God's reiteration of the Davidic Covenant to Solomon. Amidst this monologue is found the often-misused conditional terms of judgment and restoration during the Monarchy period under the Mosaic Covenant:

> If I shut up the heavens so that there is no rain, or if I command the locust to devour the land, or if I send pestilence among My people, and My people who are called by My name humble themselves and pray, and seek My face, and turn from their wicked ways, then I will hear from heaven, will forgive their sin, and will heal their land (7:13-14).

In context, these terms of judgment, repentance, and restoration are specifically for Israel under the dispensation or economy of the Mosaic Covenant, and are not transferrable to any other people group or time.

Chapters ten through the conclusion of the book recount the history of the Divided Kingdom including the fall of kingdoms, the exile, and Cyrus' decree authorizing the first return (36:22-23). It is notable that the last three verses of the book are repeated at the beginning of the book of Ezra.

PSALMS

Psalms: Communion With God

1-41
Book 1: David (37), Anonymous (4)

42-72
Book 2: David (18), Sons of Korah (8),
Anonymous (3), Asaph (1), Solomon (1)

73-89
Book 3: Asaph (11), Sons of Korah (4), David (1), Ethan (1)

90-106
Book 4: Anonymous (14), David (2), Moses (1)

107-150
Book 5: Anonymous (28), David (15), Solomon (1)

Background

The five-book collection is titled *tihili'im*, meaning *praises*. The Greek *psalmoi* provides the origination of the English *psalm*. The five-part division is from antiquity, and is evidenced by the doxologies that conclude each of the first four sections. Some suggest that this division mirrors the Torah (also containing five books).

There are numerous authors, including: David (73), The Sons of Korah (including Heman, author of Psalm 88) (12), Asaph (12), Solomon (2), Moses (1), Ethan (1), as well as numerous anonymous or unattributed Psalms (49). Much of the writing occurred during the Monarchy Period, while the book was probably compiled toward the end of that age, possibly by Ezra.[10] It is alternately possible that the collection may have been compiled by Solomon, with later additions by the men of Hezekiah.[11] In either case, God has provided an inspirational body of text, preserved through the ages for His glory, and acknowledged to be inspired (Lk. 20:42, 24:44; Acts 1:20, 13:33).

Content

Just as the Torah gave God's requirements of a holy and just God, the Psalms give a very vivid portrayal of an intimate God who involves Himself in the emotions and concerns of man. The Psalms present Him as sovereign yet personal, and as wrathful yet merciful. As Psalm 19:7-9 declares,

> The law of the Lord is perfect, restoring the soul; the testimony of the Lord is sure making wise the simple. The precepts of the Lord are right, rejoicing the heart; the commandment of the Lord is pure, enlightening the eyes. The fear of the Lord is clean, enduring forever. The judgments of the Lord are true; they are righteous altogether.

The book of Psalms presents all these elements.

In addition to the standard strophe system of Hebrew poetry, the book of Psalms contains the following poetic tools, songs, and instruments, used to beautify and embellish the already powerful words of praise:

1. *psalm* – song of praise

2. *shiggaion* – from the verb, *to err*, but due to context probably a highly emotional form

3. on the *gittith* – possibly an instrument or tune that originated from Gath of the Philistines

4. on *muth-labben* – refers to the youth of a son, and may refer to the treble voice of such

5. on an eight stringed lyre

6. on stringed instruments

7. for flute accompaniment

8. *mikhtaim* – epigrammatic poem, or atonement psalm, possibly from the word for gold, *ketem*

9. prayer

10. upon *aijeleth hashshahar* – possible reference to the help of daybreak, which is illustrative of the theme of the psalm

11. *maskil* – contemplative, didactic or skillful psalm, from the verb ' to make wise'

12. for *jeduthun* – probably tune or instrument

13. according to the *shoshannim* – probably tune or instrument

14. set to *alamoth* - note 1 Chron. 15:20-21, describing eight Levites playing harps

15. according to *mahalath* – could reference a tune or instrument

16. according to *jonath elem rehoikim* – possible reference to a sacrificial dove, or simply a tune or instrument

17. set to *al-tashheth* – meaning, *do not destroy*, and could reference a tune, includes imprecatory psalms requesting retribution and deliverance from the wicked

18. according to *shushan eduth* – probably tune or instrument

19. set to *el shoshannim eduth* – probably tune or instrument

20. according to *mahalath leannoth* – probably tune or instrument

21. *song of ascents* – a pilgrimage psalm, referring to the ascent to Jerusalem

22. *selah* –pause, crescendo, or a musical interlude [12]

The Messianic Theme

The Messianic idea is a very significant part of the Psalms:

Psalm 2 – deals with the Christ, hated and rejected by the world, sovereign Judge, King, and Son, and worthy of the trust of man.

Psalm 8 – refers to the temporary humbling and ultimate exalting of the Christ, and is ascribed to Christ in Hebrews 2:6-8.

Psalm 16:10 – speaks of His resurrection (Acts 13:35).

Psalm 22 – portrayed the anguish of the Christ, as He echoed the opening words on the cross (Mt. 27:46, etc.).

Psalm 31:5 – His last words before dying (Lk. 23:46).

Psalm 34:20 – prophetic regarding His bones not being broken (Jn. 19:32-36).

Psalm 38:11-14 – addressed His silence before His accusers (Mt. 26:56, 58-63; 27:11-14, etc.)

Psalm 41:9 – refers to Christ's betrayal by Judas (Mt. 26:20-25).

Psalm 68:18 – refers to His ascension (Eph. 4:8-10).

Psalm 69 – identifies Christ's zeal for His Father's house in v. 9 (Jn. 2:17), and prophetic of events on the cross in verse 21 (Mt. 27:34, etc.).
Psalm 110 – identifies Christ as King in verse 1 (Mt. 22:44, etc.), and as Priest in verse 4 (Heb. 5:6, etc.).

From these Psalms referring to the Messiah, much information can be gleaned. Certainly the idea of a suffering Messiah is fully presented, as well as the idea of a sovereign King and an understanding Priest. This wealth of prophetic information leaves His rejectors further without excuse.

PROVERBS

Proverbs: The Wisdom of Righteousness			
Proverbs of Solomon: To His Son / 1-9	Proverbs of Solomon: To His Son	1-4	Heed Wisdom
		5	Avoid Adultery
		6	Of Diligence, Worth, & Purity
		7	Avoid Immorality
		8-9	Wisdom vs. Foolishness
	Proverbs of Solomon / 10-24	10-18	The Righteous vs. The Wicked
		19-24	General Instruction
	Proverbs of Solomon: Transcribed by Hezekiah's Men 25-29	25-26	Moral Comparatives
		27-29	General Instruction
	30	Words of Agur to Ithiel & Ucal	
	The Oracle of King Lemuel's Mother 31	31:1-9	The Excellent King
		31:10-31	The Excellent Wife

Background

Titled in the Hebrew, *sepher mish'le'i*, the meaning is literally *book of proverbs*. Several of the authors are named within the book: Solomon, Hezekiah's men, Agur, and King Lemuel. The book was probably compiled either by Hezekiah's men around 700 BC, or by a later redactor such as Ezra or the like.

Content

The purpose statement of the book appears right away:

> To know wisdom and instruction, to discern the sayings of understanding, to receive instruction in wise behavior, righteousness, justice, and equity; to give prudence to the naïve, to the youth knowledge and discretion, a wise man will hear and increase in learning, and a man of understanding will acquire wise counsel, to understand a proverb and a figure, the words of the wise and their riddles (1:2-6).

But the theme is found in the following verse: "the fear of the Lord is the beginning of knowledge; fools despise wisdom and instruction" (1:7).

The one who would seek after wisdom, must heed the instructions of these proverbs, and in so doing would learn of the fear of the Lord. That person will gain true wisdom. The Biblical worldview, predicated on the fear of the Lord, is the *accurate* worldview, according to Solomon.

The first nine chapters illustrate this concept in Solomon's proverbs to his son (and sometimes sons). Solomon addresses the issue of wisdom, both defining and identifying its true value. In addition, key issues in this section are maintaining purity, diligence, and worth. Beginning in chapter ten and continuing through chapter twenty-four is a second section, a lengthy and thorough contrasting of righteousness versus wickedness that concludes with numerous instructions and warnings on sundry topics. Chapters twenty-five through twenty-nine contain the proverbs of Solomon as transcribed by Hezekiah's men, and deal with moral similes and further moral instruction. Chapter thirty contains the obscure Agur's oracle to Ithiel and Ucal (perhaps his sons?). The oracle includes a treatise on the character of God, and numerical proverbs of morality. Finally, the thirty-first chapter is King Lemuel's recounting of his mother's oracle regarding being an excellent king and identifying an excellent wife.

As the wisest man who ever lived (1 Kin. 3:12), Solomon rightly identified that a proper perspective of Almighty God is the true essence of wisdom.   Without this perspective, the covenant promises could not truly be understood, appreciated, or enjoyed, as His character is revealed in each.

ECCLESIASTES

	1:1-11	Vanity: Nothing New
	1:12-18	Vanity: The Earthly Quest for Wisdom
	2:1-11	Vanity: Pleasure
	2:12-17	Vanity: Wisdom, Madness, Folly
	2:18-23	Vanity: Labor
	2:24-3:22	Conclusion: The Plan of God
	4:1-3	Vanity: Life
	4:4-6	Vanity: Works
	4:7-12	Vanity: Aloneness
	4:13-16	Vanity: Foolishness
	5:1-7	Conclusion: Fear God
	5:8-20	Conclusion: Enjoy the Gifts of God
Ecclesiastes: The Search For Meaning	6	Vanity: Riches, Wealth, Honor
	7-8:5	Conclusion: Advice for Life
	8:6-17	Conclusion: The Work of God
	9:1-6	Vanity: Life & Death
	9:7-10	Conclusion: Enjoy the Gifts of God
	9:11-18	Conclusion: Wisdom Better Than Strength
	10:1-11	Examples
	10:12-14	In Words
	10:15-19	In Work
	10:20-11:8	Conclusion: Advice for Life
	11:9-10	Conclusion: Rejoice
	12:1-7	Conclusion: Remember the Creator
	12:8-12	Vanity: All is Vanity
	12:13-14	Conclusion: God is Not Vanity

Background

The Hebrew title is *qoheleth*, named for the preacher who identifies himself as the author in 1:1, saying, "The words of the preacher, the son of David, king in Jerusalem." The English title *Ecclesiastes* comes from the Greek word meaning *to assemble*, and referring to the preacher's function which Solomon performed in 1 Kings 8:1.

While the statement of authorship seems quite self-explanatory, it is not without difficulty. Due to the presence of Aramaic and even Persian linguistic characteristics within the book, some suggest a very late date of writing and consequently challenge Solomonic authorship. These criticisms do not seem, however, to consider the possibility that the manuscripts we now possess today could have been copied and even translated to and from Aramaic back into Hebrew during the Exilic or Post-Exilic periods. In any case, the claim for authorship requires the author to have been a king in Jerusalem, which, if not referring directly to Solomon, then it would have been referring to a descendant of David who ruled in Jerusalem, and could have been no later than the 586 BC, a date which would not have allowed for the Persian or Aramaic influences. It seems best to conclude in agreement with Jewish tradition, that Solomon indeed did author the book during the latter part of his life, no later than around 950-935 BC.

Content

Probably the single most important factor is the repeating of the phrase *under the sun*, occurring twenty-eight times within the book. The phrase emphasizes an earth-centered perspective, and it bolsters the thesis stated in 1:2, "Vanity of vanities! All is vanity."

Solomon takes his readers on a journey in which he will state, portray, and epitomize personally the truth that without eternal perspective, life is meaningless. He confirms many of the themes in the book of Proverbs, only here he utilizes a more personal narrative approach. While his thesis is the hopelessness of life without God, his conclusion is the meaningfulness of every part of life in relation to God:

The conclusion, when all has been heard, is: fear God and keep His commandments, because this applies to every person. For God will bring every act to judgment, everything which is hidden, whether it is good or evil (12:13-14).

All too often humanity seeks to trivialize life by disregarding responsibility for our actions. In so doing we fail to acknowledge his Creator. The question of true fulfillment and happiness cannot be answered successfully in this way. Solomon provides living proof that the ways of humanity without God are empty, foolish, and fruitless. The wisest man who ever lived would have us recognize our status as humble creatures before our Creator. Only then can we truly enjoy the blessings He has prepared for us. Only then can we see Him in all His covenant-keeping glory. To fear God is to possess wisdom and knowledge.

SONG OF SOLOMON

Song of Solomon: Be Exhilarated With Her Love (Prov. 5:15-19)	1:1-4a	Bride: Longs for the Groom
	1:4b	Chorus
	1:5-7	Bride: Her Dignity
	1:8-10	Groom: Praise for the Bride
	1:11	Chorus
	1:12-14	Bride: Treasures Her Groom
	1:15	Groom: Praises Her Beauty
	1:16-17	Bride: Praises Him
	2:1	Bride: Fertile & Beautiful
	2:2	Groom: Praises Her
	2:3-6	Bride: Delights in His Affection
	2:7	Groom: Seeks Her Peace
	2:8-13	Bride: The Groom Beckons
	2:14	Groom: Her Form is Lovely
	2:15	Chorus
	2:16-17	Bride: Admires His Work
	3:1-4	Bride: Seeks & Finds Him
	3:5	Groom: Seeks Her Peace
	3:6-11	Chorus: Solomon's Wedding Day
	4:1-15	Groom: Praises Her Loveliness
	4:16-5:1	Consummation
	5:2-8	Bride: Separation
	5:9	Chorus
	5:10-16	Bride: Praises His Loveliness
	6:1	Chorus
	6:2-3	Bride: Unity & Admiration
	6:4-12	Groom: Praises Her
	6:13	Chorus
	7:1-9	Groom: Captivated by Her Beauty
	7:10-8:3	Bride: Seeks Intimacy with Him
	8:4	Groom Seeks Her Peace
	8:5a	Chorus
	8:5b-7	Love is Strong
	8:8-9	Chorus
	8:10-14	Bride: Affection & Satisfaction

Background

Titled in Hebrew, *shir hasherim*, the meaning is literally *song of songs.*   The title Song of Solomon is due to the claim of authorship found in 1:1, "The Song of Songs which, which is Solomon's." The book was written by Solomon probably between 975-950 BC.

Content

For some, the subject matter of the Song presents difficulty. If it speaks of a literal relationship, commending marital love, then it is very explicit in nature, and as a result some have shied away from a literal interpretation of the Song as an expression of physical love and affection between a man and a woman.

Two allegorical possibilities have been suggested as alternate understandings: (1) that the Song speaks of God and Israel, or (2) that the Song portrays Christ and the church. First-century Jewish tradition spiritualized the Song, relating it to God's love for Israel, with the verses of the Song tracing Israel's history in relationship to God, while the young church spiritualized it also, identifying it with Christ's love for the church.

Despite the conclusions of these traditions, there is no evidence, internal or external, to justify an allegorical interpretation. From the text itself, it seems evident that Solomon is celebrating the beauty of marital and physical love as a precious gift of God. The explicit detail regarding physical attributes and affection, for example, leaves no doubt as to the Song's meaning.

Recall the words of the same Solomon in Ecclesiastes 4:11: "If two lie down together they keep warm, but how can one be warm alone?" He again counsels his readers to,

> Let your heart be pleasant during the days of young manhood. And follow the impulses of your heart and the desires of your eyes. Yet know that God will bring you to judgment for all these things (Ecc. 11:9).

In like manner he admonishes his son with the following:

Drink water from your own cistern, and fresh water from your own well. Should your springs be dispersed abroad, streams of water in the streets: Let them be yours alone, and not for strangers with you. Let your fountain be blessed, and rejoice in the wife of your youth. A loving hind and a graceful doe, let her breasts satisfy you at all times; be exhilarated always with her love (Prov. 5:15-19).

In each of these instances, Solomon describes the importance and beauty of companionship between husband and wife, and the words of the Song only further bolster his message.

Solomon recognizes that in this life God has provided an immeasurable gift of companionship. He recognizes, perhaps through his own failings and misuses, that the wife of one's youth is to be treasured and enjoyed and that faithfulness to her is the very epitome of honor (Prov. 5,7). The Song of Solomon is a detailed example of a man and wife cherishing one another through various stages of life. It should serve as a lighthouse of sorts for marriages today.

Although the allegorical conclusions are not appropriate hermeneutically, there can be a secondary tie-in, for as the Song helps to strengthen marriages – which serve as picture of of Christ and the church (Eph. 5:31-32) – God's living illustrations (married couples) become an even more beautiful portrayal of His love, further demonstrating His superlative character.

OBADIAH   840 BC

Judgment Pronounced	For Pride Against Israel	For Violence to Israel	As Fire	As Possessors	As Judges
1-2	3-9	10-16	17-18	19-20	21
Justice to Edom: Judgment 1-16			Mercy to Israel: Exaltation 17-21		
Obadiah: The Justice & Mercy of God					

Background

The claim of authorship for the shortest book of the Hebrew Bible is found in 1:1 – "The vision of Obadiah." This is all that is said about the prophet within the book, and Obadiah is only one of two prophets (Malachi being the other) with no additional biographical information provided other than their name. Obadiah is a fairly common name in the Hebrew Bible, applying to fourteen people (including this prophet). The author does not seem to be identifiable with any of the other thirteen; therefore we know nothing of his identity and background save his name.

The timing of the prophecy implies Edomite violence toward Jerusalem, and best fits in context with the events of 2 Kings 8:20

and 2 Chronicles 21:16-17, and therefore the date of around 840 BC is ascribed. Obadiah 11 and 13 indicate something short of a complete destruction of Jerusalem, which might have otherwise indicated a later date of writing, such as 587-586 BC,[13] though it is very possible the prophecy anticipates Edomite infringement upon Israel at the time of the exile.

Content

Obadiah prophesies judgment against Edom for injustice against Israel. Recall that Edom descended from Esau, and was a source of strife with Israel. This pronouncement of judgment reminds that God would protect His covenant people Israel, and would keep His promise to Abraham that "the one who curses you I will curse" (Gen. 12:3). God's attitude of justice can be clearly seen in verse 15: "For the day of the Lord draws near on all nations. As you have done, it will be done to you. Your dealings will return on your own head." Although directed precisely at Edom, the judgment is a stern warning to all nations who would interfere with the security of God's beloved nation.

Edom's consequences would arrive with the day of the Lord, as indicated also in Malachi 1:3-5. Malachi wrote nearly four hundred years after Obadiah, and anticipated a still yet future judgment for Edom. Notice how patient God is. His timing is not necessarily our timing. Israel was to be encouraged not by the soonness of justice, but by the certainty of justice. The timing is always up to God. Trusting in Him is our responsibility.

JOEL   835 BC

1:1-14	1:15-20	2:1-11	2:12-20	2:21-27	2:28-32	3:1-17	3:18-21
Present: On Jerusalem	Judgment Coming	Judgment Described	Judgment Avoidable	Judgment Temporary	Interlude: Times of the Gentiles	Final Judgment	Final Restoration
	Near 1:15-2:27				Far 2:28-3:21		
Joel: Judgment & Restoration							

Key Promises

The Day of the Lord------------------------------Joel 1:15; 2:2, 30-3:3
The Holy Spirit Promised -------------------------------------Joel 2:28

Authorship

The author identifies himself as Joel (meaning *Yahweh is God*), the son of Pethuel. He ministered as a prophet to the Southern Kingdom of Judah around approximately 835 BC. Joel was probably the very earliest prophet to the Southern Kingdom. The early date is likely, due to the nations mentioned and the nations excluded from his prophecy (for example, Assyria is not mentioned, although Sennacharib, king of Assyria planned an attack on Judah in the days of Hezekiah, as recorded in 2 Kings 18-19), and also due to some apparent references to Joel by later prophets (e.g., Amos 1:2, quoting Joel 3:16; and Is. 13:6, quoting Joel 1:15).

Summary

These were turbulent times for Israel. The early-mid ninth-century BC brought draught and locusts. The political culture of the Southern Kingdom was still intact, but the spiritual culture was steadily failing. It was no coincidence that the land became less and less giving, as the consequences for breaking the Mosaic Covenant were physical. Joel brings from God an intense message of judgment intermingled with grace, giving elements of present and future, near and far, and indicating key eschatological elements such as the judgments and restoration of Israel, along with the times of the gentiles.

Joel begins with an appeal for the inhabitants of every class in the land of Judah to remember back even to the days of the elders' fathers. He asks "has anything like this happened?" He challenges his audience to think upon the significance of the events taking place, and he details an invasion of locusts – one of epic severity. Four swarms of locusts invaded and were destroying the nation's agriculture, a plight that would lead to famine.

It is important to realize that Joel is describing literal events, not painting an allegory. The invasion is presented as literal, and while prophecy can make use of present tense terminology in describing future events, in that type of usage there is always in the context an analogy that connects the terminology to the future. Here there is none. Also, the manner in which these events are described lends evidence to their historicity. Joel makes no use of allegorical language that would imply anything other than a literal event.

Joel connects the calamity to its cause: he reminds the people that they are God's people. He calls them to wail as a woman betrothed yet without her bridegroom — reminding them of their marriage covenant with God (expounded in Jer. 31:32; Is. 54:5). Joel observes that because rain is being withheld, the vegetation is dried up. Note Joel's emphasis on grain, wine, and oil for offering — these in particular are not available. He says that "the grain offering and the libations are withheld from the house of your God" (1:13b). Encouraged by the wicked leadership of people like Jehoram, Ahaziah, and Athaliah, Judah had been unfaithful to God. She had taken part in all kinds of idolatry, worshipping the false gods of every nation with which she came into contact.

Just as was prophesied in Leviticus 26 and Deuteronomy 11 and 28, God would use the land as a means to judge His faithless people. God's use of the land to bless and judge Israel was a cornerstone of the Mosaic Covenant, a covenant that Israel had violated. God had called down judgment upon Judah and her land because of her sin, and was now calling the people, through Joel, to humble themselves and pray.

Joel 1:15; 2:2, 30-3:3
The Day of the Lord

The present judgment was merely a precursor to a more significant and severe judgment by God. In 1:15 Joel introduces one of the most profound events in Biblical prophecy – the Day of the Lord: "Alas for the day! For the day of the Lord is near and it will come as destruction from the Almighty." The Day of the Lord encompasses "any period of time however long or short that involves God's direct judgment on the world."[14] Specifically this is a reference to a definite future time which will begin the tribulation, will include Christ's Second Coming, and will conclude with His Millennial Kingdom.

It is concluded that the day of the Lord will include the time of the tribulation. Zechariah 14:1-4 makes it clear that the events of the second coming are included in the program of the day of the Lord. II Peter 3:10 gives authority for including the entire millennium age within this period.[15]

Joel illustrates with clarity that the aspect of the Day to which he refers is a time of future tragedy for Israel, a time that will later be clarified by Jeremiah as "Jacob's Trouble" (Jer. 30:7). With the assurance of coming judgment, Joel paints a horrific picture. He describes the Day of the Lord as a day of darkness and gloom – an event of terror. He describes a great invasion that will be thorough in its destruction of Judah. He seems to be describing an invasion of locusts in terrifying hyperbolic terms, but he does not say that the invaders are locusts as he did in chapter one. This description emphasizes the invading army being under the authority of God. Note that the invading army of chapter two is described with frequent simile that is absent in the description in chapter 1.

> The locust army is regarded as a foretaste of an invading army in the day of the Lord, i.e., in the tribulation period. The future references may be to the demon locusts described in Revelation 9:1-12 and or to the invasion of the king of the North (Ezek. 38:15, Dan. 11:40)[16]

Joel is describing a day when the judgment of God will be complete, his purpose being to draw Judah into repentance. He calls the nation to return to the Lord with a repentant spirit – "Rend your hearts, not your garments" (2:13). God sought a spiritual humbling. Here would come into play the promise of 2 Chronicles 7:13-14. Even in a severe time of judgment, God presented an opportunity for grace. If Judah would repent, her land would be restored. And even after the future judgment was to come, God would still restore Judah, and ultimately Israel. But before that restoration would come remarkable displays of God's greatness and judgment:

> And I will display wonders in the sky and on the earth blood, fire, and columns of smoke. The sun will be turned into

> darkness, and the moon into blood before the great and awesome day of the Lord comes (2:30-31).

This passage is quoted by Matthew 24:29, describing events immediately preceding the coming of the triumphant Messiah King.

Joel 2:28
The Holy Spirit Promised

> And it will come about after this that I will pour out My Spirit on all mankind.

Peter connects this promise *in kind* to the coming of the Holy Spirit at Pentecost, which signified the birth of the church (Acts 2:16-21). While the scope of this promise extends beyond this singular event (the specific pouring out of 2:28 comes after the initial aspects of the day of the Lord), the prophetic dominoes had begun to fall. The coming of the Spirit and the birth of the church signified the beginning of the last days, which would find their completion in the day of the Lord. At this day, judgment would be completed and Israel would finally know her full restoration under her triumphant Messiah King.

JONAH   780 BC

Jonah's Call	Jonah's Rebellion	Jonah's Discipline	Jonah's Repentance & Deliverance	Nineveh's Repentance: God's Mercy	Jonah's Anger	God's Rebuke of Jonah
1:1-2	1:3	1:4-17	2	3	4:1-3	4:4-11

Jonah: God's Mercy To The Gentiles: Nineveh

Background

The author is identified in 1:1 as Jonah, the son of Amittai. He ministered during the reign of Jeroboam II of the Northern Kingdom around 780 BC (2 Kin. 14:25).

Content

Jonah was called by God to present a message of repentance and forgiveness to Nineveh, the magnificent capital city of the Assyrian Empire. Jonah responded to God's mercy toward gentiles by disobeying that call. Rather than going east to present God's gracious opportunity to the inhabitants of Nineveh, Jonah fled west to the seaport of Tarshish (in modern day Spain). God promptly judged Jonah's disobedience, causing a great storm to endanger the ship on which Jonah sailed. The crew members recognized Jonah's guilt and cast him overboard. God's judgment was not without grace, however, as God provided a large sea creature to ingest Jonah and relocate him after his apparent death (2:2,5,6). The creature transported Jonah to safety, releasing him to dry land.

Again, God called Jonah to go to Nineveh, and this time Jonah submitted, proclaiming God's message to Nineveh. The people of Nineveh responded humbly with repentance, and God showed them mercy. Jonah responded once again to God's grace, resenting God for showing mercy to gentiles. He admitted to fleeing the first time due to fear that God would show them mercy, saying, "for I knew that Thou art a gracious and compassionate God, slow to anger and abundant in lovingkindness, and one who relents concerning calamity" (4:2).

These words are almost a verbatim quote of Exodus 34:6. Jonah knew that God's character was consistent. In response, God provided Jonah with a unique object lesson. As Jonah watched over the city to observe whether or not God would judge it, God provided a plant for Jonah's shelter. Then God brought a worm that destroyed the plant, taking away Jonah's comfort and making him angry. God rebuked Jonah with these words:

> Do you have good reason to be angry about the plant?... You had compassion on the plant for which you did not work, and which you did not cause to grow, which came up overnight and perished overnight. And should I not have compassion on Nineveh, the great city in which there are more than 120,000 persons who do not know the difference between their right and left hand, as well as many animals (4:9-11)?

With these words God demonstrated His care even for the gentiles. Still, eventually the city of Nineveh fell back into its evil ways, even in violence against Israel. The prophets, Nahum and

Zephaniah, brought a new message of God's unavoidable judgment to Nineveh (Nah. 1-3, Zeph. 2:13-15). Just over a hundred years after taking the Northern Kingdom of Israel in conquest (721 BC), Nineveh and the entire Assyrian Empire fell at the hands of Nebuchadnezzar of Babylon with the Medes and Scythians in 612 BC.[17]

The Sign of Jonah

Completing Israel's rejection of her Messiah in Matthew 12, the scribes and Pharisees demand from Jesus a sign, and He responds saying:

> An evil and adulterous generation craves for a sign; and yet no sign shall be given to it but the sign of Jonah; for just as Jonah was three days and three nights in the belly of the sea monster, so shall the Son of Man be three days and three nights in the heart of the earth. The men of Nineveh shall stand up with this generation at the judgment, and shall condemn it because they repented at the preaching of Jonah; and behold something greater then Jonah is here (Mt. 12:39-41).

Jesus references Jonah and the events of Jonah as a twofold sign condemning Israel's unbelief and unrepentance. The first component was that Jonah's stay in the belly of the whale portrayed Christ's burial. The second was that even the wicked people of Nineveh repented at the preaching of Jonah, while that generation of Israelites would reject the message of their own Messiah.

AMOS   755 BC

Amos: Judgment On Nations & Israel	1-2:3 Judgment on Nations	1:1-2	Introduction
		1:3-5	Damascus
		1:6-8	Gaza
		1:9-10	Tyre
		1:11-12	Edom
		1:13-15	Ammon
		2:1-3	Moab
	2:4-9:15 Judgment on Israel	2:4-5	Judah
		2:6-5:3	Israel
		5:4-15	Judgment Still Avoidable
		5:16-20	The Day of the Lord
		5:21-27	God Rejects Israel
		6	God Judges Israel's Arrogance
		7	Amos Intercedes & Amaziah Rejects
		8-9:10	Judgment Unavoidable
		9:11-15	Restoration Assured

Key Promise

The Silent Years --Amos 8:11

Background

The author identifies himself as Amos, a sheepherder from Tekoa (five miles southeast of Bethlehem). Amos ministered during the reigns of Uzziah king of Judah and Jeroboam II king of Israel. Also he mentions that his prophetic ministry occurred two years prior to the great earthquake mentioned in Zechariah 14:5.

Although the exact date of the earthquake is not known, the book is dated around 755 BC, during that latter reign of Jeroboam II. The calling of Amos is recorded in 7:14-15, as God pulled Amos from his occupation of being a herdsman and grower of sycamore figs, and thrust him into the prophetic ministry with the command to "Go prophesy to my people Israel."

Content

Amos' primary ministry was to the Northern Kingdom, although his prophecy begins with numerical oracles of judgment ("for three transgressions and for four...") on various afflicters of Israel. He focuses on the failures of Israel and the coming judgment as consequence for those failures. Amos' prophecy particularly focuses on Israel's violation of the Mosaic Covenant, stating in 2:4, "they have rejected the Torah of Yahweh."

At the outset, this judgment is still avoidable, as the Lord says, "Seek Me that you may live" (5:4,6,14). However, the prophetic message of repentance is rejected (7:10-13), and from then on judgment is assured: "Moreover, Israel will certainly go from its land into exile" (7:17b). Included in that promise of exile would be a period of silence, a famine for God's word: "Behold, days are coming," declares the Lord, "When I will send a famine on the land, not a famine for bread or a thirst for water, but rather for hearing the words of the Lord" (8:11).

It appears that with the conclusion of Malachi's ministry God kept that promise. God did not speak through any prophet again until the coming of John the Baptist, who came as a forerunner to the Messiah, just as had been prophesied by Malachi.

Amos' prophecy concludes with a message of hope and restoration. God would keep His word. Israel would go into exile. God would be silent for a time. But then, God would be earnest in showing His mercy, and would ultimately restore the fortunes of Israel through the restored house of David (9:11).

HOSEA   750 BC

1-2:13 Hosea's Commission: A Family of Harlotry: Israel's Unfaithfulness Portrayed	2:14-23 Israel's Restoration	3 God's Faithfulness Portrayed	4-6 Israel's Unfaithfulness	7-13 Israel's Guilt & Judgment	14 Israel's Restoration

Hosea: God is Faithful Despite Israel's Unfaithfulness

Background

The author identifies himself as Hosea the son of Beeri, and he dates his ministry during the reigns of Uzziah, Jotham, Ahaz, and Hezekiah, kings of Judah, and Jeroboam II, king of Israel. His ministry covers a span of roughly sixty years. The book is best dated around 750 BC. Hosea was a resident of the Northern Kingdom (7:5), and his prophetic ministry focuses on that territory. His ministry would prove to be God's last warning to the Northern Kingdom before her destruction in 721 BC, as Hosea was the last prophet ministering to the Northern Kingdom.

Content

Hosea's focus is on Israel's unfaithfulness to the Mosaic Covenant. God uses him as a living portrayal of that unfaithfulness, commanding him to "take a wife of harlotry; for the land commits flagrant harlotry" (1:2). Hosea is obedient and takes Gomer, the daughter of Diblaim, as his wife. The difficulties Hosea encounters in this marriage mirror God's difficulties with unfaithful Israel.

The theme of God as faithful husband to an unfaithful Israel is echoed throughout, and as a result of Israel's unfaithfulness, judgment is pronounced. Yet, even in the midst of judgment, God maintains that there will be a future restoration: "I will heal their apostasy, I will love them freely" (14:4). Hosea also underscores that Israel's restoration would include a return to submission to the house of David, and that in the last days Israel would seek her Messiah King (3:5). Of Messianic note is 11:1: "When Israel was a youth I loved him, and out of Egypt I called My son." At first glance, this seems a casual reference to the nation of Israel and the exodus from Egypt. However, Matthew attributes the reference to the young Christ's flight to Egypt as protection from the evil plot of Herod (Mt. 2:15).

MICAH   725 BC

Exile of Israel & Judah	God Will Preserve Israel	Judgment: Leaders, Priests, Prophets	The Last Days: The Just Judge	The Deliverer From Bethlehem	Israel's Unjustifiable Unfaithfulness	Acceptable Offerings to God	Judgment of Israel	The Evil of Israel	Judgment & Restoration of Israel
1	2	3	4 -5:1	5:2-15	6:1-5	6:6-8	6:9-16	7:1-6	7:7-20

Micah: Israel's Judgment & Hope

Background

The author identifies himself as Micah of Moresheth, a city roughly twenty miles west of Jerusalem. His prophetic ministry focused on the Southern Kingdom, and spanned the reigns of Jotham, Ahaz and Hezekiah, kings of Judah. The judgment upon the North is referred to as still in the future, so the bulk of the book was authored before 721 BC, most likely very near that date, probably 725 BC.

Content

Micah's prophecy addresses primarily Judah, and Samaria to a lesser degree. It is notable that Micah does not provide a warning *to* the inhabitants of the Northern Kingdom, but rather provides God's pronouncement of judgment *concerning* the territory. Micah particularly addresses the failed leadership – both spiritual and political, the false prophets, priests, and the heads and rulers. God's judgment would be particularly stern with them.

God's plan of restoration is also described, as the last days judgment and restoration of Israel are considered in chapter four. As always, God's plan of restoration centers on the Messianic hope, which is again mentioned in 5:2-5a:

> But as for you, Bethlehem Ephrathah, too little to be among the clans of Judah, from you One will go forth for Me to be ruler in Israel. His goings forth are from long ago, from the days of eternity...and He will arise and shepherd His flock... and this One will be our peace.

Matthew records that the chief priests and scribes recognized this to be a reference to Messiah (Mt. 2:5-6). Even before the exile judgment on Israel, God had already provided the Israelites with the hope of restoration and the knowledge of a coming Messiah – to suffer and redeem, and to restore the nation as King.

ISAIAH   740-680 BC

Isaiah: The Salvation of God – The Holy One of Israel	1-39	Rejection By God	1-6	Condemnation, Consummation, & Commission
			7-12	Coming of Messiah
			13-23	Condemnation of Nations: Oracles/Burdens
			24-27	Coming Tribulation & Triumph
			28-33	Condemnation (Woes) & Consummation
			34-35	Condemnation & Consummation
			36-39	Chronicle of Mercy
	40-66	Restoration By God	40-48	A Sovereign Redeemer
			49-57	A Servant Redeemer
			58-66	A Ruling Redeemer

Key Promise

The Messiah: Suffering Servant and King ---------------------Is. 53

Background

Isaiah identifies himself as the son of Amoz. He describes his ministry as taking place during the reigns of Uzziah, Jotham, Ahaz, and Hezekiah. These were all kings of Judah, the territory in which Isaiah ministered (1:1). His ministry spanned roughly sixty years, from about 740-680 BC. Jewish tradition held that he was a member of a royal family, and that he was violently killed during the reign of Manasseh as a result of his godly ministry.[18]

Because of the predictive nature of Isaiah's ministry, some modern (as early as the late eighteenth century) critics have promoted a documentary theory regarding the authorship of Isaiah. These critics postulate that in addition to the historical Isaiah, who authored the first thirty-nine chapters, there was a redactor living in Babylon after the fall of Jerusalem who completed the latter part of the book (thereby justifying prophetic mentions of the coming fall of the city). This redactor is commonly referred to as Deutero-Isaiah. Some even refer to a third author, Trito-Isaiah. These conclusions are unwarranted and have the effect of denying that Isaiah's were legitimate predictive prophecies.

Despite these more recent higher-critical conclusions Jewish tradition as well as New Testament writers acknowledge the genuineness of Isaiah's authorship. Matthew attributes Isaiah 40:3 and 42:1 to Isaiah (Mt. 3:3, and 12:17-18). Luke recognizes Isaiah's authorship of 40:3-5 (Lk. 3:4) and 53:7-8 (Acts 8:28). Paul acknowledges that Isaiah wrote the latter portion of the book, attributing Isaiah 53:1 and 65:1 to Isaiah (Rom. 10:16,20). Christ also further confirmed the legitimacy of Isaiah's authorship, quoting both the earlier section of the book (Is. 29:13 in Matthew 15:8-9) and the latter part of the book (Is. 61:1 in Mt. 11:5) as authentic and predictive.

Content

Chapter six records the call of Isaiah and also provides an important description of the character of God. In both the Hebrew and Greek languages, repetition is a significant tool for emphasis. Isaiah 6:3 contains the only description of God that is repeated three times in immediate succession: "Holy, holy, holy, is the Lord of Hosts." The angels who are acquainted with His character echo those words here. The same description is also recorded in Revelation 4:8, this time spoken by the four living creatures before His throne. To understand God and His plan, we must recognize the centrality of His holiness. His attributes – love, mercy, wrath, justice – are rooted in holiness.

Chapters one through thirty-five record a detailed message of judgment upon Israel and the nations, interspersed with an equally powerful message of restoration. Chapters thirty-six through thirty-nine contain a historical interlude, recounting the invasion and miraculous defeat of the Assyrians led by Sennacherib in 690 BC, as well as the merciful healing of Hezekiah. This narrative is a parallel to 2 Kings 18-20 and 2 Chronicles 32. Chapters forty through sixty-six further advance the prophecies of Israel's restoration, with special emphasis on the Messiah.

The Messianic Message

While Isaiah's prophecy contains the messages of judgment and ultimate restoration, his is primarily a Messianic prophecy. Some important Messianic passages include: 1:18 (salvation by Messiah), 7:14-16 (Messiah's virgin birth), 9:1-7 (the Light of the World and the Prince of Peace), 11 (the Shoot of Jessie and His coming Kingdom), 40 (His forerunner, the Word, the Shepherd, the Sovereign), 42:1-7 (the gentleness of Messiah and His ministries of the Covenant and of healing), 50:5-8 (the abuse of Messiah before His crucifixion), 52:13-15 (His appearance, redeeming work, and ultimate glorification), 53 (the suffering Messiah who would pay for sin), and 61:1-3 (Christ read this passage in the temple and attributed it to Himself [Lk. 4:18].).

ZEPHANIAH   625 BC

On Jerusalem	Opportunity for Salvation	On Philistia	On Moab & Ammon	On Ethiopia	On Assyria	On Jerusalem	On Nations	Of Nations	Of Israel
1	2:1-3	2:4-7	2:8-11	2:12	2:13-15	3:1-7	3:8	3:9-10	3:11-20
1-3:8 Day of Wrath								3:9-20 Day of Restoration	
Zephaniah: The Day of the Lord									

Background

Zephaniah was in the royal line of Judah – a descendant of Hezekiah (the son of Cushi, son of Gedaliah, son of Amariah, son of Hezekiah). His ministry takes place during the reign of Josiah king of Judah. The book of his prophecy is appropriately dated around 625 BC. During Zephaniah's ministry King Josiah led Judah in a national revival. Josiah was considered the most righteous king in Judah's history (2 Kin. 23:25). However, it was not enough to stay the wrath of God that arrived just a few years after Josiah's reign.

Content

Zephaniah's prophecy focuses on the Day of the Lord (as he repeats the phrase more than ten times), emphasizing the two elements of that same Day: wrath and restoration. In addition to Israel, the nations of Philistia, Moab, Ammon, Ethiopia, and Assyria are all judged under the coming day of wrath. Of these nations, only Israel is promised an eternal restoration.

NAHUM   650-612 BC

1:1-8 Character of God	1:9-14 Corruption of Nineveh	1:15-3:4 Character of Judgment	3:5-15 Capacity of Judgment	3:16-19 Certainty of Judgment
The Proclamation 1:1-14		The Explanation 1:15-3:19		
Nahum: Judgment by A Just God				

Background and Content

The author identifies himself as Nahum the Elkoshite (1:1), most likely referring to the town of Elcesei,[19] which was between Jerusalem and Gaza. Nahum is the second of three (also Jonah and Obadiah) prophets whose recorded ministries were directed toward nations other than Israel. Titled *the oracle of Nineveh* (1:1), Nahum's prophecy was directed at the capital city of the Assyrian Empire while it still maintained its strength.

The city, symbolizing the entire nation, was condemned for plotting evil against the Lord (1:11). Specifically the judgment comes as vengeance (1:2) for Assyria's oppression of Israel and Judah (1:15). This prophecy shows again that God will not tolerate wickedness, and in keeping His Abrahamic Covenant, evils against His people will not go unpunished (Gen. 12:3). The prophetic judgment came upon Nineveh in 612 BC. The city was destroyed completely by the Medo, Babylonian, and Scythian alliance. This destruction was thorough and spelled the end of the Assyrian Empire.

HABAKKUK   609 BC

Habakkuk: The Sovereignty of God	1:1-4	1st Petition: Why is Wickedness not Judged?
	1:5-11	God's Answer: Judgment Coming (Chaldeans)
	1:12-2:1	2nd Petition: Why Use the Wicked to Judge?
	2:2-20	God's Answer: The Five Woes
	3	Prayer of Habakkuk: God is Sovereign

Background

The author is identified only by his name and office (1:1). No further biographical information is given. Due to references to the Chaldeans (1:6,15) and the imminence of their arrival, it is evident that Habakkuk's writing took place shortly before the first Chaldean (or Babylonian) invasion in 605 BC, and probably shortly after King Josiah's death in 609 BC.

Content

This dialogue between God and Habakkuk gives great insight into the purposes of God. First, Habakkuk, bemoaning Israel's unfaithfulness to the Mosaic Covenant (1:4), questions God's justice and seeming lack of intervention. God responds, explaining that judgment would come quickly and severely at the hands of the Chaldeans, who God prepared beforehand. God shows He is not inactive, nor does His plan falter.

Again, Habakkuk questions how God can use such a wicked nation as His tool to correct Israel. God responds by proclaiming five woes against the wicked, and against Babylon. God's explanation of His direction of human events is quite simple: "Let the earth be silent before Him" (2:20b). Reminiscent of Paul's explanation of the sovereignty of God (Rom. 9:20-21), God's response to Habakkuk is such that the only appropriate response was one of praise and prayer.

JEREMIAH   627-586 BC

Jeremiah: Old Covenant Consequences & New Covenant Hope	Judah's Last Days 1-23	1	Appointment of Jeremiah
		2-3:10	Israel's Unfaithfulness
		3:11-4:18	Call to Repentance
		4:19-6:30	Coming Judgment
		7-9	Judgment Proclaimed
		10	The Foolishness of Idolatry
		11	The Covenant Broken
		12	Jeremiah's Prayer
		13-17	The Pride & Failures of Judah
		18-20	Persecution of Jeremiah
		21-23	Message to Kings & Prophets
	Jerusalem Under Siege 24-38	24-26:6	Prophecy Regarding Exile
		26:7-24	Persecution of Jeremiah
		27-30	Prophecies of Exile & Return
		31	The New Covenant
		32-33	Restoration Assured
		34	Judgment of Zedekiah
		35	Obedience of the Rechabites & Disobedience of Judah
		36	The Scroll of Jeremiah
		37-38	Persecution of Jeremiah
	Jerusalem Falls 39-52	39-45	Fall of Jerusalem & Jews in Egypt
		46-50	Judgment of Nations
		51	Judgment of Babylon
		52	Fall of Jerusalem & Exile

Key Promises

Background

Jeremiah identifies himself as the son of Hilkiah, of the Priests of Anathoth in Benjamin (1:1). He was both priest and prophet. He was assisted in his writing by Baruch, who functioned as Jeremiah's secretary (36:4). Jeremiah identifies his ministry as commencing during the reign of Josiah, the righteous king of Judah, and continuing until the exile of Jerusalem. His ministry to the Southern Kingdom of Judah started early in his life, while he was still a youth (1:6), and continued for a period of over forty years.

Content

Like the prophet Isaiah, Jeremiah also includes historical narrative within his prophetic message: his own imprisonment and opposition to his message (20, 26, and 32), the response of Hananiah to God's prophecy of exile (28), the reading of the Law, Jeremiah's imprisonment under Zedekiah (36-38), the fall of Jerusalem and flight to Egypt of some Jews (39-45), and the recounting of the fall of Jerusalem (52). Jeremiah's message to Judah was that judgment via exile was assured and submission to the invaders was commanded (27). This was an unpopular message, and Jeremiah was persecuted for it. However, he had been prepared beforehand to deal with the opposition he would face (1), a reminder that God prepares His people for the tasks He gives them (Eph. 2:10).

Jeremiah 25:1-14; 29:10
The 70-Year Exile

God pronounced upon Israel, and specifically Judah, a precise seventy-year exile as a consequence for breaking the Mosaic Covenant. The seventy-year period would allow the land to enjoy the Sabbath years that Israel had failed to keep while dwelling in it (Lev. 25-26). But after this period, Israel would be restored to her land.

The initial siege of Nebuchadnezzar against Jerusalem and consequent exile took place in 605 BC, while the first return under Zerubbabel occurred in 537-536 BC, and thus the political exile was seventy years. As of 520 BC the exile was considered by Zechariah to still be continuing. Zechariah 1:12 seems to indicate that this exile specifically referred to the destruction of the temple in 586 BC, and its restoration in 516 BC – thus encapsulating a spiritual exile.

Serving as the last prophet before and during one of the most severe periods of judgment in Israel's history, Jeremiah was used of God to bring the most profound message of hope the world could ever know. God keeps His promises.

Jeremiah 30:7
Jacob's Trouble

Jeremiah provides a further glimpse of the far aspect of God's judgment on Israel: "Alas! For that day is great, there is none like it, and it is the time of Jacob's distress, but he will be saved from it." He discusses God's purpose for what will be later identified by Daniel (Dan. 9) as Israel's seventieth week, and by Jesus (Mt. 24) as the (great) tribulation. It will be a final refining of Israel as she prepares for the second coming of her Messiah King.

Jeremiah 31:27-40
The New Covenant

This promise is critical to God's keeping of His unconditional covenants. The Abrahamic and Davidic Covenants both describe an eternal people and an eternal kingdom, but neither of them deals specifically with the problem of sin. That problem would seem to render the keeping of these covenants to be impossible. Neither of those covenants specifically address the allusion to redemption in Genesis 3:15. Neither of them specifies how eternal life is attained. The Mosaic Covenant certainly didn't address these things either, as it simply served to magnify the failings of man and the need for redemption. However, the journey of the Hebrew Bible climaxes with this promise:

> 'Behold, days are coming', declares the Lord, 'when I will make a new covenant with the house of Israel and with the house of Judah, not like the covenant which I made with their fathers in the day I took them by the hand to bring them out of the land of Egypt, My covenant which they broke, although I was a husband to them,' declares the Lord. 'But this is the covenant I will make with the house of Israel after those days,' declares the Lord, 'I will put My law within them, and on their heart I will write it; and I will be their God, and they shall be My people. And they shall not teach again each man his neighbor and each man his brother ,saying, 'Know the Lord,' for they shall all know Me ,from the least of them to the greatest of them,' declares the Lord, '**for I will forgive their iniquity, and their sin I will remember no more**' (31:31-34).

There are five key elements revealed in the New Covenant:

1. *It would be made with Israel specifically.* This was a precisely aimed covenant that would only apply to Israel.

2. *It would be characterized by spiritual life and an intimate knowledge of God.* In contrast to the Mosaic Covenant, which was

primarily national in scope, this would be an individual *and* a national covenant, dealing uniquely with individual responsibility and individual knowledge of and fellowship with God. It would be universally effectual on all of Israel.

3. *It would result in the forgiveness of the individual sins of the Israelites.* This covenant would not simply provide a temporary atonement or covering for sin, rather it would eliminate them by virtue of forgiveness. Yet, God, in His justice would not simply sweep the sin under the rug. As pictured by the ram in the thicket at Isaac's deliverance (Gen. 22), Christ would be the substitutionary Sacrifice for sin (Is. 53), in order that God could forgive the offenders of their sin.

4. *It would include the elements of physical restoration of the nation (31:27-30; 31:38-40).* In fulfillment of the Abrahamic and Davidic Covenants, there would be a lasting people, restored to her land for eternity.

5. *It would be fulfilled after Jacob's Trouble.* While the covenant is ratified, or activated, by Christ through His blood (Mt. 26:26-29), the covenant would not be fulfilled until the second coming of the Messiah King.

It is worth noting here that the New Covenant is to be fulfilled exclusively by Israel and Judah, so it is distinctly Jewish. Nonetheless, God accounted for gentile salvation in the Abrahamic Covenant, when He said, "in you all the nations of the earth shall be blessed" (Gen. 12:3). Through the same blood that paid for Israel's New Covenant, gentiles also may receive God's forgiveness (Eph. 3:1-5). Whereas Israel has many promises, the promise for Jews and gentiles in the present age is eternal life in Christ and through His blood (1 Jn. 2:25).

5

Promises Delayed

Exile

605-536 BC – Political Exile

586-516 BC – Spiritual Exile

Prophetic Books

Lamentations	Ezekiel	Daniel

Key Promises

The Coming Kingdom -----------------------------------Ezek. 37-48

The Timeline ---Dan. 9

LAMENTATIONS 586 BC

1 Weeping for Israel	2 Judgment: Thorough & Deserved	3:1-18 Jeremiah Laments Judgment	3:19-66 Jeremiah Hopes in God	4 Judgment Detailed	5 Jeremiah Prays for God's Mercy

Lamentations: Weeping for Israel

Background

The sixth book of the ketuvim is titled *e'kah* in the Hebrew, meaning *how*, from the first word of the text. The Vulgate added a subtitle: "the Lamentations of Jeremiah the prophet."[20]   While there is no internal statement of authorship, the evidence supports Jeremiah's authorship: the timeframe and nature of Jeremiah's ministry, a possible reference to the book in 2 Chronicles 35:25, and the agreement of Jewish tradition.

Content

The book consists of five poems (one per chapter) in acrostic form. The first mourns the exile (1:3) and the fall of Jerusalem from favor (1:17). The second acknowledges the deserved anger of God (2:1). The third is in two thematic parts. First, Jeremiah personalizes the judgment, mourning his own loss (3:7-13). He then rejoices at the goodness of the Lord (3:22-23). The fourth poem recounts vividly the horrors of the siege and the destruction of Jerusalem (4:10). In the final poem, Jeremiah prays for mercy and his pleas for restoration. Jeremiah penned these words in the midst of the greatest turmoil of his lifetime: "The Lord's lovingkindnesses indeed never cease, for His compassions never fail. They are new every morning; Great is Thy faithfulness" (3:22-23). Even when God's mercies were not evident in circumstances, Jeremiah takes Him at His Word, and draws powerful hope from His promises.

EZEKIEL   593-570 BC

Ezekiel: Judgment & The Kingdom Hope	**1-36:21** **Visions of Judgment**	1	5th year:	Ezekiel's Visions of God
		2-3		Appointment of Ezekiel
		4-5		Judgment of Jerusalem Portrayed
		6		Idolatry Judged
		7		Wickedness Judged
		8-9	6th year:	Vision of Abomination & Judgment
		10		God's Glory Departs the Temple
		11:1-13		Leadership Judged
		11:14-25		Return From Exile Promised
		12		Exile Portrayed
		13		Judgment on False Prophets
		14:1-11		Call to Repentance for Idolatry
		14:12-15:8		Judgment & Restoration of Jerusalem
		16		God's Grace to Unfaithful Israel
		17		2 Eagles & The Vine: Consequences of Unfaithfulness
		18		Individual Responsibility
		19		Lamentation for the Princes of Israel
		20	7th year:	God's Grace to Unfaithful Israel
		21		God's swords of Judgment
		22		Israel's Wrongdoing
		23		Oholah & Oholibah: Unfaithfulness
		24	9th year:	Fall of Jerusalem: Arrival & Portrayal
		25-32	9th-12th year:	Judgment on Nations
		33:1-20		Ezekiel the Watchman
		33:21-33		Jerusalem's Fall
		34		Judgment of Shepherds & God's Care for His Sheep
		35-36:21		Judgment on Mt. Seir & Blessings on Mountains of Israel
	36:22-48:35 **Visions of Hope**	36:22-38		Israel's Restoration
		37:1-14		Dry Bones: The Ingathering
		37:15-28		A United Kingdom
		38-39		Invasion & Judgment of Gog: 7 Oracles
		40-47:13	25th year:	The Kingdom Temple
		47:14-48:35		The Land of the Kingdom

Key Promise

The Coming Kingdom ---------------------------------------Ezek. 37-48

Background

Ezekiel identifies himself as "the priest, son of Buzi" (1:3). Like Jeremiah he filled roles as both priest and prophet. His prophetic ministry began at age thirty (1:1), in the fifth year of the exile of Jehoiachin (597 BC). The prophecy of Ezekiel begins in 593 BC. Ezekiel was one of the deportees of this second deportation (the first, in 605 BC, and the third, in 586 BC). His visions begin near the river Chebar in Chaldea. Even rationalistic critics have not questioned Ezekiel's authorship, until recently. Modern criticisms are generally based on two suppositions.

First, since the book is divided into two sections – one of judgment, and one of blessing – two authors must have been involved. This theory is as ridiculous as it sounds, and it discounts God's use of His prophets to communicate multi-faceted messages (judgment and restoration) in many other instances. Second, many of the prophecies (e.g., 11:13) seem to be written from the perspective of someone living in Judah, while Ezekiel claimed to have lived as an exile in the Chaldean territories. This criticism also discounts several logical explanations. First, news of events (such as 11:13) could have reached Ezekiel fairly quickly. Also God could have easily shown the prophet the events as they were happening (as He did with other prophets such as Daniel and the apostle John). After all, the visions were supernatural to begin with.[21]

Content

God's purpose is not difficult to identify, as the book is characterized by the repetition of the phrase *then they shall know that I am the Lord* (or a form of the phrase) some fifty times. Certainly, God sought to cause the nation to see that He was indeed the covenant keeping God, that He had judged Israel justly, and that He would restore Israel mercifully just as He had promised.

Ezekiel's prophecy is traced chronologically throughout the book, beginning in his fifth year of exile, as he recounts a grand vision of God, and his appointment as a prophet to the soon to be exiled peoples of Israel. His fifth year prophecies continue through chapter seven, as the thorough judgment and destruction of Jerusalem is prophesied.

Ezekiel's sixth year brings another prophecy of judgment spanning chapters eight through nineteen and encompassing vivid portrayals of Jerusalem's impending destruction, including God's Glory leaving the temple (ch. 10). Even amidst this judgment, God would remember His covenant with Israel. He would establish a new and everlasting covenant for Israel's eternal restoration (16:60-63). Chapters twenty through twenty-three cover Ezekiel's seventh year, and provide pronouncement and portrayal of God's final judgment of the nation. The ninth year of exile brought a renewed siege of Jerusalem. After just less than six months of horror-filled siege, Jerusalem was utterly destroyed (2 Kin. 25:1-21), and the prophecies of judgment were fulfilled. Ezekiel's prophecies shifted in focus from Israel to the nations that had afflicted them in the past, as he proclaimed judgment upon the nations in chapters twenty-five through thirty-two. Chapters thirty-three through thirty-six brought the conclusion of the twelfth year prophecies of Ezekiel as watchman, judgment upon the leaders of Israel, judgment upon nations, and the beginning of the message of hope for Israel. The message of restoration gains momentum in 36:22-38, as Ezekiel speaks of a physical restoration (36:24), then a spiritual restoration (36:27), and introduces the coming Kingdom.

Ezekiel 37-48
The Coming Kingdom

One of the most amazing panoramas of Biblical prophecy is recorded in Ezekiel 37-48. Ezekiel recounts his vision of the valley of the dry bones (ch. 37), a portrayal of the future ingathering of the nation to her land. He also speaks of the restoration of the Davidic Kingdom. It is worthy of note to point out that the Kingdom consists of physical restoration first, and spiritual restoration second – in contrast to the allegorical conclusions of replacement theology (that the church replaces Israel), which suggests spiritual domination of the church first, followed by a physical return and reign of Christ – a view inconsistent with Biblical eschatology.

But before Israel would enjoy eternity in her restored Kingdom, there would be a confederacy of nations that would come against Israel as described in chapters thirty-eight through thirty-nine: Persia (modern day Iran), Ethiopia (the Sudan), Put (a nation next to Persia), Gomer (modern day Germany), and Beth Togarmah (Armenia, possibly Turkey and Siberia). This confederacy is led by "Gog of the land of Magog, the prince of Rosh, Meshech, and Tubal" (38:2-3). Magog, Tubal, and Meshech are identified as sons of Japheth (Gen. 10:2). Gog's location is in the "remote parts of the north" (38:15 & 39:2).   Some suggest plausibly that this confederacy led attack on Jerusalem will occur before the second coming of Christ, and while this is certainly possible, it seems more likely to be the climax of Satan's final rebellion after the Millennial Kingdom (Rev. 20:8-9). In both passages (Rev. 20:8-9 and Ezek. 38:6) the fire of God wins the victory.

Chapters forty through forty-eight record the literal measurements of the Kingdom temple and the literal boundaries of the Kingdom land. This references the Millennial reign of Christ (Rev. 20). In the context of the Millennial Kingdom, there is question about the purpose for the renewed sacrificial system, since the blood of animal sacrifices can never remit sins (Heb. 10:4) and therefore, the Millennial system of sacrifice has nothing to do with issues of sin and forgiveness. It is also important to recognize that the promises of the Kingdom were not based on the conditional Mosaic Covenant which included animal sacrifice, but rather on the unconditional Abrahamic, Davidic, and ultimately New Covenant. The sacrifices of the Mosaic Covenant would point forward, prefiguring in memorial roughly 1400 years to the sacrifice of Christ. The sacrifices during the Millennium would point back in memorial of that same sacrifice. Each age has a memorial, whether prefiguring or remembering back to the cross of Christ. The Mosaic age had the animal sacrifices of the Mosaic Covenant. The church age has the Lord's Supper (which will also continue in the Kingdom, see Mt. 26:29). The Kingdom will have both.

The amount of time that will have passed between Christ's sacrifice and the commencement of the Millennial Kingdom is more than two thousand years, and such a span would certainly warrant this type of memorial. It is also possible that the sacrifices during the Millennium are related to Israel's national ceremonial cleansing – serving as a national or ceremonial atonement, rather than an individual one. In any case, the coming of the Kingdom was assured, and the promise offered hope to repentant Jews who found themselves exiled from their land.

DANIEL   605-536 BC

Daniel: The Timeline of the Ages	1	Daniel, Hananiah, Mishael, & Azariah
	2	Nebuchadnezzar's Dream: The Great Statue: Babylon, Medo-Persia & Greece, Rome, Kingdom of God
	3	Nebuchadnezzar's Image: Shadrach, Meshach & Abadnego
	4	The Humbling of Nebuchadnezzar
	5:1-30	Belshazzar's Feast, Condemnation, & Demise
	5:31-6:28	Daniel Under Darius: The Lions Den
	7	The 4 Beasts: 4 Kings & the 10 Horn Kingdom
	8	The Ram & The Goat: Medo-Persia & Greece
	9	Daniel's Prayer & God's Response: 70 Weeks
	10	Daniel's Vision of Truth & Conflict
	11:1-39	Truth & Conflict: Rise & Fall of Kings
	11:40-12:8	The End Time
	12:9-13	Final Words to Daniel

Key Prophetic Issue

The Timeline --Dan. 9

Background

Daniel, a youth of noble blood (1:3-4), was taken captive in Nebuchadnezzar's first conquest of Jerusalem in 605 BC and ministered in Babylon for roughly seventy years. As he completes the book, he is aged and told to prepare for death (12:13). The best date for the completion of the book is 536 BC, as his final visions occurred in the third year of the reign of Cyrus of Persia (10:1), who ruled from 539-530 BC. Due to the amazing precision of Daniel's prophecies, critics have suggested a later date of 167 BC, citing the book's placement in the *ketuvi'im* rather than the *nebi'im*. This conclusion overlooks the fact that Daniel did not minister as a prophet as did those writers in the *nebi'im*; rather, he was a head of state serving under the Chaldeans. Keil says of the book of Daniel,

> Its place in the canon among the Kethubim corresponds with the place which Daniel occupied in the kingdom of God under the Old Testament; the alleged want of references to the book and its prophecies in Zechariah and in the [apocryphal] book of Jesus Sirach is, when closely examined, not really the case: not only Jesus Sirach and Zechariah knew and understood the prophecies of Daniel, but even Ezekiel names Daniel as a bright pattern of righteousness and wisdom.[22]

There are other internal issues that have concerned critics, such as the presence of Greek-influenced terms within the text. However archaeology (particularly in the remains of Nineveh) has evidenced that Greek influence was felt even before Daniel's time.[23] Also of concern is the seeming error of Daniel 1:1 which identifies Nebuchadnezzar's invasion as being in the third year of Jehoiakim, while Jeremiah 46:2 indicates it took place in Jehoiakim's fourth year. This is easily explained by the difference between the Jewish and Chaldean calendars. Jeremiah likely wrote from the perspective of the Jewish calendar, while Daniel wrote from the perspective of the Chaldean calendar. The book of Daniel is difficult for some to accept, as it describes in great detail the future of the world, communicated with precision and purpose. The prophecies in the book find their ultimate fulfillment in the Kingdom of Jesus Christ.

Content

Daniel begins the book describing the favor and provision of God (1:9, 17-20) that enabled him to arrive at his esteemed position. In chapter two, Daniel applied his ministry of 'understanding' (1:17) to Nebuchadnezzar's dream. The dream was a vision of a great statue, the head was fine gold (symbolizing the first kingdom, Babylon), the breast and arms were silver (symbolizing Medo Persia), the belly and thighs were bronze (symbolizing Greece), and the legs were of iron (symbolizing Rome), with the feet partly iron and partly clay (symbolizing a divided Rome). The statue was crushed by an uncut stone (which symbolized the kingdom of Messiah).

Nebuchadnezzar responded favorably toward Daniel but did not humble himself before God, as evidenced by his construction of a golden image of himself in chapter three. Nebuchadnezzar demanded nationwide worship of the statue, prompting God's protection of Shadrach, Meshach, and Abednego from the fiery consequences they received for breaking this edict. The Babylonian king temporarily humbled himself before God, but was ultimately disciplined by God in chapter four on account of his arrogance, after which time he humbled himself and honored the Lord.

Chapter five records the arrogance and debauchery of Belshazzar, and the judgment that was pronounced on him by God's handwriting on the wall. Chapter six, emphasizing the fulfillment of the prophecy regarding Belshazzar's demise and the ultimate conquest of the Babylonians by the Medo-Persians (5:25-28), records Daniel's service to Darius the Mede, including the account of God's protecting Daniel from the lions in the lions' den.

Chapter seven continues Daniel's visions of the ages, as he sees a vision of four beasts, symbolizing the four kingdoms to reign before Messiah. The fourth beast (Rome) had ten horns, symbolizing ten kingdoms (divided Rome) that would arise.

Another horn devoured three of the horns, and it became exceedingly great for three and a half years before it would be judged and overthrown by Messiah. This stunning vision refers to antichrist's dominance over a new restored yet divided Rome, and his ultimate defeat by Christ.

The panoramic visions continue in chapter eight. This time Daniel sees a ram with two horns (Medo-Persian) that was shattered by a goat with one conspicuous horn (Greece, led by Alexander the Great). The goat grew arrogant, and the horn was broken, and four horns came up in its place (referring to the division of Alexander's kingdom between his four generals). One of the horns grows exceedingly great. From it comes the fourth kingdom and the prince (another reference to antichrist) who magnifies himself, equating himself with the Lord of Hosts. This prince stops sacrifice in the temple and causes transgression for twenty-three hundred days, or six years and one hundred and ten days. This is roughly six months short of the seven-year period prophesied for the period of the tribulation, and it most likely takes into account the time necessary to set up the sacrificial system at the beginning of the seven-year period.[24]

Daniel 9
The Timeline: Daniel's 70 Weeks

Chapter nine finds Daniel examining the prophet Jeremiah's declarations of a seventy-year exile (Jer. 25:14, 29:10), and responding humbly to the Lord in prayer, as the time of the exile was drawing to a close. The personal humility that Daniel demonstrates in his prayer is exemplary. Ezekiel describes him as one of three most righteous men in Scripture (Ezek. 14:14, 20). God holds Daniel in such high regard that before Daniel even concludes his prayer, the angel Gabriel is sent to provide an answer to his prayer. Gabriel speaks to Daniel regarding the timeline of future events:

> Seventy weeks have been decreed for your people and your holy city, to finish the transgression, to make an end of sin, to make atonement for iniquity, to bring in everlasting

righteousness, to seal up vision and prophecy, and to anoint the most holy place (9:24).

The seventy weeks is literally seventy *sevens* (*heptamades* in the Greek), and refers to seventy Sabbaths of years (Lev. 25:8), or four hundred and ninety years. There are two elements of purpose, with six specific results:

Dealing with sin

1. to finish the transgression

2. to make an end of sin

3. to make atonement for iniquity (Christ at the cross)

Dealing with righteousness

4. to bring in everlasting righteousness (Jer. 23:5-6; 31)

5. to seal up vision and prophecy – *to seal* in the sense of royal authentication, fulfilling God's plan

6. to anoint the most holy – either referring to the temple or the Messiah

> So you are to know and discern that from the issuing of a decree to restore and rebuild Jerusalem until Messiah the Prince there will be seven weeks and sixty two weeks; it will be built again, with plaza and moat, even in times of distress (9:25).

The first 7 weeks (49 years) probably references the remaining years of Old Testament prophetic ministry after the decree of King Artaxerxes in Nehemiah 2:1-6 (the only decree pertaining to the actual city),[25] while the following 62 covers the intertestamental period (434), which includes the 400 years of silence (Amos 8:11).

Prophetic Math

This adds up to a total of 483 years of 360-day years (according to the Jewish lunar calendar). According to the sun calendar, years are made up of 365 days. The lunar calendar would add a 13th month to make up the difference when enough days had accumulated, but this addition is not characteristic of Biblical prophecy (see Rev. 11:2,3; 12:6; 13:5), so five days per year must be subtracted to fit into the lunar calendar. 5 days x 483 years = 2415 extra days, or roughly 6 2/3 years.

Here is the formula: 445 BC + 483 years = 38 AD – 6years (for the lunar calendar adjustment) = 32 AD, which would complete the 7 and 62 weeks of years.

> Then after the sixty-two weeks the Messiah will be cut off and have nothing, and the people of the prince who is to come will destroy the city and the sanctuary. And its end will come with a flood; even to the end there will be war; desolations are determined (9:26).

There is historical consensus that Christ was crucified in 33 AD (fulfilling the first part of this prophecy), and that Rome destroyed Jerusalem in 70 AD (fulfilling the second). Thus the first 483 years of the 490-year schedule is completed.

> And he will make a firm covenant with the many for one week, but in the middle of the week he will put a stop to sacrifice and grain offering; and on the wing of abominations will come one who makes desolate, even until a complete destruction, one that is decreed is poured out on the one who makes desolate (9:27).

The people who destroyed Jerusalem were Rome, and therefore the prince would be a Roman prince, presiding over the ten-kingdom confederacy of Rome. He will make a seven-year covenant, which he will break in the middle of its term, bringing about extreme destruction and ultimately being destroyed himself. This describes the activity of antichrist during the tribulation period immediately prior to the second coming of Messiah. The final seven-year period of this prophecy commences with the prince's covenant, so the timeline has paused for some time, awaiting his arrival on the scene. The purpose for this gap is later explained in Romans 9-11. Imagine Daniel's amazement. He had sought the Lord for an end to the exile, and God provided him with the timeline to the ultimate restoration of Jerusalem.

Conclusion

Daniel's visions continue in chapter ten, as he sees a terrifying vision, the details of which he does not record. The prophecy of chapter eleven describes later events of Persia and Greece with such detail and precision that liberal critics contend that the book was written after the events had already taken place. Chapter twelve concludes Daniel's visions with a message of encouragement from Michael the archangel, as he describes the future salvation and restoration of God's people. Daniel asks how long until the wonders are completed, and Michael responds by saying "a time, times, and a half a time" (12:7), referring to the latter three and a half years of the tribulation. This is the time of great tribulation described in Matthew 24.

Daniel seeks hope in the Lord at the outset of chapter nine. God explains His purpose for revealing His plan. It is a plan that gives hope, as it reminds us that He is sovereignly in control of all earthly events, and His plan is being fulfilled to the letter. His promises are true, and we can trust in Him, for He is our Hope.

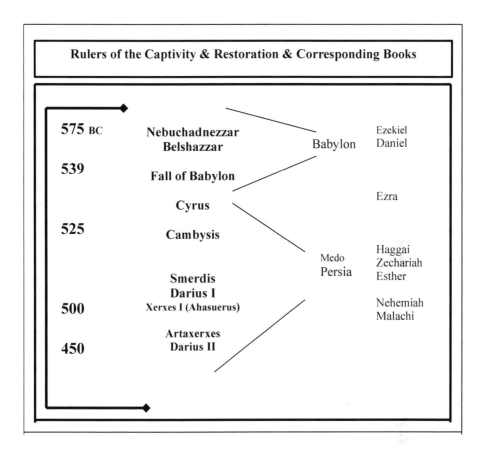

Rulers of the Captivity & Restoration & Corresponding Books

6

Promises Kept

Return and Restoration

538-400 BC

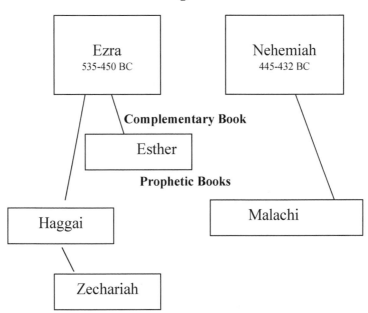

Chronological Books

Ezra
535-450 BC

Nehemiah
445-432 BC

Complementary Book

Esther

Prophetic Books

Haggai

Malachi

Zechariah

Key Fulfillment

Exile Ended: Completion of the Temple --------------Ezra 6:13-15

Key Promise

The Forerunner, Messiah, and Judgment --------------Mal. 3:1-6

EZRA   538-450 BC

Ezra: Spiritual Restoration – The Temple	1st Return: Zerubbabel 1-6	1	Cyrus Decree for Temple Restoration
		2	Census of the Returning Exiles
		3:1-7	Festivals & Sacrifices Resumed
		3:8-13	Temple Restoration Begun
		4:1-16	Temple Restoration Opposed: Shimshei & Rehum
		4:17-24	Artaxerxes Decree to Cease Temple Restoration
		5	Temple Restoration Resumed Despite Opposition
		6:1-13	Darius Sanctions Temple Completion
		6:14-22	Temple Completed, Dedicated, & Utilized
	2nd Return: Ezra 7-10	7	Artaxerxes Decrees Ezra's Return
		8:1-20	Census of the Returning Exiles
		8:21-36	God Provides a Safe Return
		9	Israel's Sin of Intermarriage
		10:1-17	Israel's Restitution
		10:18-44	Census of Those Who Intermarried

Key Fulfillment

Exile Ended: Completion of the Temple --------------Ezra 6:13-15

Background

Originally the book was combined with Nehemiah in the Hebrew canon. Ezra, a descendant of the priestly line of Aaron (7:1-3), and as a scribe skilled in the Law (7:6), has traditionally been regarded as the author. The division of the two books was first made in the Latin Vulgate, and has since become common. The book covers historical events occurring between the years 538-450 BC. As Ezra was probably the author of the Chronicles, they were most likely completed during this timeframe as well.

Summary

Chapters one through six recount the first return of Israel from exile under Zerubbabel in 537-536 BC, numberings of those exiles returning, and the completion of the temple in 516 BC. That latter event concluded the seventy-year exile as prophesied in Jeremiah (25:14; 29:10), precisely seventy years after the temple was destroyed (586 BC). Chapters seven through ten record the second return, this time under Ezra, in 458 BC. This return focused on the spiritual restoration of the exiled nation, as they recommitted themselves to obedience to God. The book of Ezra provides further evidence of God's faithfulness to His promises as the history of Israel continued to unfold.

HAGGAI   520 BC

1:1-4 Problem: Disobedience / Temple Neglected	1:5-6 Result: Judgment / Israel Neglected	1:7-8 Command: Obedience / Build Temple	1:9-11 Alternative: Judgment / Neglect of Israel	1:12-15 Obedience: / Temple Construction Begun	The Obedient Have Hope / God is Faithful	The Obedient are Holy / Israel Must be Holy	The Obedient are Blessed / Blessing of Zerubbabel
1st Word 1:1-15					2:1-9 2nd Word	2:10-19 3rd Word	2:20-23 4th Word

Haggai: Word of Renewed Obedience

Background

Haggai the prophet (1:1) is the author. His ministry is linked with Zechariah's (Ezra 5:1), although Haggai's ministry predated Zechariah's by about two months (Hag. 1:1, Zech 1:1). The dating of his writing is evident, as Haggai postscripts each of the four sections of the book. A date of 520 BC is most likely.

Content

The returning exiles encountered significant opposition in their attempts to rebuild the temple, and the work had come to a stop (Ezra 4). Chapter one recounts God's call to continue the work, and the obedience of Haggai and Zerubbabel to that call. Less than two months later, another word of the Lord came to Haggai, this one a message of encouragement based on the faithfulness of God. Two months later, a third word of the Lord came to Haggai, this time a call to purity and a promise of blessing. On that same day, the Lord gave Haggai a message of future blessing for Zerubbabel. The temple project was completed, on God's timetable, in 516 BC.

ZECHARIAH   520-518 BC

Zechariah: Israel's Hope of Redemption	Visions 1-6	1:1-3	Admonition to Repentance
		1:4-6	Example of the Fathers
		1:7-11	Four Horses Patrolling the Earth
		1:12-17	Restoration of Israel Coming
		1:18-21	4 Horns & 4 Craftsmen
		2	Restoration of Jerusalem Coming
		3	Joshua the High Priest
		4	Golden Lampstand & 2 Olive Trees
		5:1-4	The Scroll
		5:5-11	The Ephah
		6:1-8	Four Chariots of Patrol
		6:9-15	Offering for the Crown
	Words 7-8	7	Inquiry of Bethel & Call to Obedience
		8	Restoration of Israel Coming
	Burdens 9-14	9:1-7	Judgment on Nations
		9:8-11:3	Future Deliverance of Israel
		11:4-17	The Doomed Flock & The Worthless Shepherd
		12:1-9	War & Defense of Jerusalem
		12:10-14	Israel Mourns Her Messiah
		13	Judgment of False Prophets
		14:1-8	The Coming of the Lord
		14:9-11	The Kingdom of the Lord
		14:12-21	Judgment on Nations

Background

The author is Zechariah the prophet, the son of Berechiah, the son of Iddo (1:1). His ministry to the returned exiles began two months after Haggai's (Hag. 1:1, Zech 1:1), and continued for at least two years, dating the prophecy from 520-518 BC (although some suggest a slightly later completion date of 480 BC, due to the mention of Greece in 9:13. This is a possibility, but certainly not a necessity).

Content

Zechariah's prophecy is divided into three sections: visions, words, and burdens. The visions are found in chapters one through six, as God shows Zechariah visions of the restoration and blessing of Jerusalem. Two years later, the word of the Lord came to Zechariah concerning an inquiry of the men of Bethel about true worship, a call to obedience, and the coming prosperity of Israel.

The burdens, or oracles, discuss judgment on nations, restoration, and future uniting of Israel (ch. 9-10). The burden of chapter eleven includes a judgment on the doomed flock and a foolish shepherd. This prophecy interestingly mentions thirty shekels of silver, alluding to the price the flock placed on the Good Shepherd (Zech. 11:12-13; Mt. 26:15; 27:3-10).

The burden of chapter twelve includes a reference to God's pouring out of His Spirit, in order that Israel may weep for the Messiah they have pierced (12:10-11). As a result, false prophets are judged (ch. 13) for leading the people away from Messiah, yet God will ultimately defend Jerusalem, defeat her enemies, and rule all the earth as the Faithful King (ch. 14).

ESTHER

Esther: God Protects His Covenant People	1:1-9	King Ahasuerus' Banquet
	1:10-22	Queen Vashti's Deposing
	2:1-20	Queen Vashti's Replacement: Esther (Hadasseh)
	2:21-23	Mordecai Uncovers an Assassination Plot
	3	Haman's Plot & Edict to Destroy the Jews
	4:1-3	Mordicai Uncovers Haman's Plot
	4:4-17	Esther's Intercession
	5:1-8	Esther's Banquet
	5:9-14	Haman's Hatred of Mordecai
	6:1-9	Ahasuerus Remembers Mordecai
	6:10-14	Haman's Humiliation & Mordecai's Exaltation
	7	Esther's Petition & Haman's Demise
	8:1-7	Mordecai Honored
	8:8-17	Ahasuerus' Decree: Self-Defense For the Jews
	9:1-18	The Jews Are Victorious
	9:19-32	The Jews Remember: The Feast of Purim
	10	The Greatness of Mordecai

Background

We can't be certain who wrote Esther. Nehemiah is a possibility, although Mordecai seems the most likely candidate.[26] The book was written sometime shortly after 473 BC, the year the Feast of Purim was established in remembrance of God's protection of Israel.[27] Some doubt the authenticity of the book due to its lack of a single mention of God, but the thematic elements of Esther strongly emphasize God's sovereign protection of His covenant people.

Summary

In the reign of Ahasuerus (elsewhere identified as Artaxerxes I), Queen Vashti rejects an inappropriate command to appear before the king and his guests (1:10-12). The king is angered and ultimately replaces her with a lovely Jewish woman named Esther (Hadasseh), who had managed to keep her heritage a secret from the king (2:20). During that time Mordecai, Esther's cousin, uncovered a plot, and saved the king's life, and while his act was recorded in the records, he received no reward (2:21-23).

Later, Haman, one of the king's royal officials, was angered by Mordecai's refusal to bow down before him. This led Haman to create an edict for the destruction of the Jews (ch. 3). Esther learns of the plot, and plans a banquet to present her case to the king (ch. 4-5). In the meantime, Haman builds a gallows upon which to have Mordecai hung, but the king, after reading the account of how Mordecai saved the king's life determines to honor Mordecai and requires Haman to publicly honor Mordecai (ch. 6). Esther informs the king of her heritage and Haman's plot against the Jews, resulting in Haman's execution upon the gallows he built for Mordecai (ch. 7). The king then honors Mordecai, and gives provision for the Jews to defend themselves (ch. 8). Upon mounting a successful defense, the Jews instituted the Feast of Purim (after the *pur*, or lot that Haman cast for the destruction of the Jews in 3:7).

The book of Esther records God's miraculous provision for the survival of His people. In order for Him to keep His word, the Jews must survive. The book acknowledges Sovereign control and purpose in human events, as evidenced by Mordecai's statement to Esther: "And who knows whether you have attained royalty for such a time as this?" (4:14). God will protect His people, and will judge those who come against them, just as He promised (Gen. 12:3).

NEHEMIAH 445-433 BC

Nehemiah: Political Restoration - Jerusalem	1-7:4 Walls Restored	1	Nehemiah's Prayer
		2:1-8	Artaxerxes Sanctions Nehemiah's Return
		2:9-20	Sanballat's Opposition
		3	Builders of the Wall
		4:1-8	Sanballat's Opposition
		4:9-23	Opposition Thwarted
		5:1-13	Usury Stopped
		5:14-19	Nehemiah's Leadership
		6:1-14	Opposition: Sanballat, Tobiah, & Geshem
		6:15-7:4	Wall Completed Despite Opposition
	7:5-13:31 Commitment Restored	7:5-73	Census of the 1st Return
		8:1-12	Remembrance & Convocation: Ezra & Nehemiah
		8:13-18	Israel Observes the Feast of Booths
		9:1-37	Israel Repents
		9:38-10:39	Israel's Covenant: Commitment to the Law & Temple
		11:1-19	Leaders in Jerusalem
		11:20-36	Cities of Judah, Benjamin, & The Levites
		12:1-26	Priests & Levites of the 1st Return
		12:27-30	Dedication of the Wall of Jerusalem
		12:31-43	The Choirs of Jerusalem
		12:44-47	Portions For Singers, Levites, & Sons of Aaron
		13	Israel's Preparation & Purification

Background

Originally united with Ezra as one book in the Hebrew canon, the Vulgate separated the two, the latter of which was authored by Nehemiah, the son of Hacaliah (1:1). He served as governor for the returned exiles from 445-433 BC (5:14). The events of Nehemiah begin in 445 BC (2:1) and conclude twelve years later (13:6).

Summary

Chapters 1-7:4 recount the restoration of the wall of Jerusalem, despite opposition from Sanballat and others. This completes the physical and political restoration from exile. Chapter 7:5-13:31 recount the restoration of the returned exiles' commitment to God, as proper worship is restored. Nehemiah is chronologically the final historical book of the Hebrew Bible. The book focuses on Israel's return and political restoration from exile. God had kept His promise to deliver a remnant from the exile in Babylon, and He would keep His other promises relating to the future Kingdom of Israel. But first would come one final prophetic messenger (Malachi), who would look to the coming preparations for Messiah, and then would come the years of silence (Amos 8:11), the famine for new revelation during the intertestamental period.

MALACHI   450-400 BC

Israel's Failures & Future Hope	1:1-5	God's Plan for Jacob & Esau
	1:6-2:9	Sin & Judgment of the Priests
	2:10-16	Unfaithfulness of Israel
	2:17-3:6	Coming Justice
	3:7	Israel's Turning Away
	3:8-12	Israel's Failure in Tithing
	3:13-15	Israel's Arrogance
	3:16-18	Israel's Remembrance
	4	Israel's Future & The Day of the Lord

(center label: **Malachi:**)

Key Promise

The Forerunner, The Messiah, & Judgment ------------Mal. 3:1-6

Background

The final prophetic messenger of the Old Testament identifies himself simply as Malachi (1:1). Archer lists the evidence for a mid-fifth century authorship:

> (1) the temple had already been rebuilt and Mosaic sacrifice reinstituted (1:7, 10;3:10)...(3) The sins which Malachi denounces are the same as those Nehemiah had to correct during his second term, namely (a) priestly laxity (1:6; Neh. 13:4-9), (b) neglect of tithes, to the impoverishment of the Levites (3:7-12; cf. Neh 13:10-13), (c) much intermarriage with foreign women (2:10-16; cf. Neh. 13:23-28). It is reasonable to assume that Malachi had already protested

against these abuses in the years just preceding Nehemiah's
return; hence a fair estimate would be about 435 BC.[28]

Content

Contradicting the newfound commitment Israel proclaimed in
the latter times of Nehemiah, Israel had failed to turn completely
from the very errors of which she repented during Nehemiah's day.
Particular judgments and warnings came to the priests for their
unfaithfulness (1:6-2:9), and to the people for their failures in
attending to the matters of God's house: specifically, their failure
to tithe (3:8-12). But as was characteristic of God in His mercy,
against the backdrop of discipline appeared the promise of future
hope.

Malachi 3:1-6

The Forerunner, Messiah, and Judgment

The first promise is of a coming messenger (3:1) who would
prepare the way for Messiah. Christ ascribes this role to John the
Baptist (Mt. 11:10). The second is of the coming Messiah, who
would sit as judge (3:2-4). The third is of certain judgment and
refining that Messiah would bring (3:5-6). Israel had been through
much in the Old Testament years. God had fulfilled or advanced
every promise He had made, and now, as Israel looked forward to
four hundred years without new revelation from God, they had the
assurance of hope, the promise of a forerunner who would
announce Messiah. God keeps His promises.

7

Promises Distinguished

Israel and the Church

Israel: The Eternal **Promises**

Genesis 12:1-3 - Abrahamic Covenant
Deuteronomy 30:1-10 - Land Covenant
II Samuel 7:8-17 - Davidic Covenant
Jeremiah 31:27-40 - New Covenant

Daniel 9 - The 70 Weeks of Israel Prophecied
Matthew 12 - Israel rejects her Messiah

EARTHLY

The Church: **The** Eternal Promise

Romans 9-11

Veiled Allusion

Genesis 12:3c - Blessing to the nations
Jeremiah 31:34b - Forgiveness of sin
Joel 2:28 - Holy Spirit predicted
John 16 - Holy Spirit promised

Direct Revelation

Matthew 16:13-20 - First prophecy of the church
Acts 2 - Birth of the church
Ephesians 1-3,5 - The mystery of the church
Galatians 3-4 - The economy of the church
I John 2:25 - The promise defined
Revelation 1-3 - The conclusion of the church
I Thessalonians 4:13-18 - the rapture of the church

HEAVENLY

Revelation 4-18 - Jacob's Trouble:
The Tribulation (Daniel's 70th
week)

(church in heaven)

Revelation 19 - The King Comes

Revelation 20 - The Kingdom
Revelation 21-22 - Eternity

Revelation 19 -Christ returns
with His bride
Revelation 20 - The Kingdom
Revelation 21-22 - Eternity

The Importance of Hermeneutics
(Biblical Interpretation)

There have historically been primarily two schools of Biblical interpretation: (1) the allegorical, and (2) the literal. Dating back to Philo (Jewish philosopher at Alexandria during the time of Christ), Origen (late 2nd century church leader), and Augustine (late 4th – early 5th century church leader), the church allegorized that which it did not understand. There are two basic tenets of the allegorical method: (1) prophecy is often interpreted allegorically, and (2) Israel has therefore been replaced in the plan of God.

A system of theology known as Covenant Theology sprung from this allegorical method, acknowledging two basic covenants: (1) works – made with and broken by Adam and continued with Israel, and the covenant of (2) grace, which replaced the old covenant, and is expressed in the church. Another group of interpreters hold to a literal interpretation of Scripture – including prophecy. This leads to a dispensational view of God's plan, summarized as follows:

> Dispensationalism is that system of theology which: views the world as a household run by God. In this household-world God is dispensing or administering its affairs according to His own will in various stages of revelation in the process of time. These various stages mark off the distinguishably different economies in the outworking of His total purpose, and these economies are the dispensations.[29]

The presupposition of the allegorical method is that God does not have plans for Israel's physical blessing in the future, due to Israel's rejection of her Messiah. To those who hold to this presupposition (as did Philo, Origen, and Augustine), the allegorical method is necessary for understanding Biblical prophecy. A literal method would result in a dramatically different understanding. The interpretation of the allegorical method and Covenant Theology is that ethnic Israel is finished as a chosen vessel of God. She had her chance and failed, and now it is the church's turn, and since the gates of hell shall not prevail against the church, she shall not suffer the same fate as did Israel. Rather she shall endure faithfully to the end, prevailing over her enemies. Under this presupposition, God's calling of Israel is not irrevocable (as Rom. 11 declares it to be).

One implication of replacement theology is that since the church replaces Israel, she has the same authority God gave Israel, and now the church can use any means necessary to prevail throughout the world. History has witnessed this error in action with the Crusades, the Inquisition, and to some extent, even the Holocaust. Anti-Semitism in the church is easily accommodated by replacement theology, Covenant theology, and the allegorical method.

There are three eschatological perspectives within Covenant Theology: the premillennial, the postmillennial, and the amillennial. Each are named for their interpretation of the timing of Christ's Second Coming. Covenant premillennialism (Christ returns before the millennium) is perhaps closest to dispensationalism, in the assertion that there is to be a kingdom of God on earth after the second coming of Christ. It differs from dispensationalism by asserting that the present and future focus is on the church, and that Israel will be excluded as a national entity. Covenant postmillennialism (Christ returns after the kingdom starts) recognizes a kingdom on earth, to be initiated by the church. Israel as a nation is not part of that kingdom. Covenant amillennialism (no millennium) considers there to be no future literal kingdom, but instead there resides a present spiritual kingdom in the hearts of believers. Again, as a nation Israel is excluded.

Dispensationalism takes a different view than Covenant theology. The literal interpretation of Scripture derives the conclusion that God is not at all finished with Israel, but rather He has only temporarily set the nation aside, in order that the gentiles might be saved as well. Through the literal grammatical-historical method of Biblical interpretation, dispensationalism recognizes a future premillennial return of Christ, a kingdom involving national Israel, and (usually) a pretribulational rapture of the church. Regarding Israel, Paul says in Romans 11:1, "I say then God has not rejected His people, has He? May it never be!" It is evident that Paul did not expect a replacement of Israel.

Much confusion exists because of the failure to carefully define, distinguish, and compare the church and the kingdom. Based on Augustine's City of God, the equation of the church and the kingdom resulted in the absolute authority of the church on earth. Postmillennialism builds the earthly kingdom on the growth and success of the church. The mistaken concept of theonomy sees the church's mission as establishing the Old Testament Law of God in the kingdoms of the world today.[30]

Dispensational theology acknowledges the literal, eternal, and unconditional nature of the covenants God made with Israel, and interprets their fulfillments accordingly. This is the logical conclusion of a literal interpretation of Scripture.

Dispensations: Number and Purpose		
12 - Doxological	7 - Soteriological	3 - Kingdom
1. Planning: Eternity Past - Jn. 17:24; Eph. 1:4; 1 Pet. 1:20		
2. Prelude: Innocence of Man - Gen. 1:1-3:5	1. Innocence: Gen. 1:3-3:6	
3. Plight: Failure of Man - Gen. 3:6-6:7	2. Conscience: Gen. 3:7-8:14	1. Preparation: Begins Gen. 3:15
4. Preservation & Provision: Common Grace & Human Govt. - Gen. 6:8-11:9	3. Government: Gen. 8:15-11:9	
5. Promises Pronounced: Gen. 11:10-Ex. 18:27	4. Promise: Gen. 11:10-Ex. 18:27	
6. Prerequisite Portrayed: The Broken Covenant (Tutor) - Ex. 19:1-Mal. 4:6 (Gal. 3:24-25)	5. Law: Ex. 19:1-Jn. 14:30	
7. Promises Proffered: The Kingdom Offered - Mt. 1:1-12:45		
8. Postponement & Propitiation: Kingdom Postponed & New Covenant Ratified - Mt. 12:46-Acts 1:26		
9. Participation: Church Age - Acts 2:1- Rev. 3:22	6. Grace: Acts 2:1 – Rev. 19:21	2. Participation: Begins Acts 2
10. Purification: Tribulation, Jacob's Trouble - Rev. 4:1-19:10		
11. Promises Performed: Kingdom Initiated - Rev. 19:11-20:6	7. Millennium: Rev. 20:1-5	3. Consummation: Begins in Rev. 19
12. Postscript: Eternity Future - Rev. 20:7 – 22:21		

Dispensational Distinctions

In order to fully grasp the promises of God, it is important to understand the dispensational distinction between Israel and the church. Misidentifying the roles which God has for Israel and those He has for the church results in an inability to understand God's plan of the ages and as a result, His character. The two (Israel and the church) are neither one in identity, nor are they one in purpose. The chief end of man is indeed to glorify God. However, God clearly uses different people in different ways to bring glory to Himself. In regards to the distinction of Israel and the church, Chafer says,

> Apart from the right understanding of this subject there can be no conception of the heavenly purpose of God in and through the Church in contrast to His earthly purpose in Israel, no conception of the divine purpose in the present age, no basis for a true evaluation of all those new realities and relationships which were made possible and established through the death and resurrection of Christ, no worthy comprehension of the present ministries of the Spirit of God, and no sufficient basis of appeal for the God-honoring life and service of the believer.[31]

In Chafer's estimation, without understanding this distinction, we cannot begin to comprehend, in essence, what Paul calls "every spiritual blessing" (Eph. 1:3) with which the church has been blessed in Christ. The scope of this distinction far transcends even eschatological issues. *This distinction is pivotal in understanding every aspect of Biblical theology.*

Pentecost recognizes God's covenants with Israel as the building blocks of eschatology:

> The covenants contained in the Scriptures are of primary importance to the interpreter of the Word and to the student of eschatology. God's eschatological program is determined and prescribed by these covenants and one's eschatological system is determined and limited by the interpretation of

them. These covenants must be studied diligently as the basis of Biblical eschatology.[32]

And again, Pentecost's lengthy comment is worthwhile here:

Chafer has set forth twenty four contrasts between Israel and the church which show us conclusively that these two groups can not be united into one, but that they must be distinguished as two separate entities with whom God is dealing in a special program...[from Chafer, Systematic Theology, Vol IV, p. 47-53]...These contrasts may be outlined as follows:(1) The extent of Biblical revelation: Israel - nearly four fifths of the Bible; Church - about one fifth. (2) The divine purpose: Israel - the earthly promises of the covenants; Church - the heavenly promises in the gospel. (3) The seed of Abraham: Israel - the physical seed, of whom some become a spiritual seed; Church - a spiritual seed. (4) Birth: Israel - physical birth that produces a relationship; Church - spiritual birth that brings relationship. (5) Headship: Israel - Abraham; Church - Christ. (6) Covenants: Israel - Abrahamic and all the following covenants; Church - indirectly related to the Abrahamic and new covenants; (7) Nationality: Israel - one nation; Church - from all nations. (8) Divine dealing: Israel - national and individual; Church - individual only. (9) Dispensations: Israel - seen in all ages from Abraham; Church - seen only in the present age. (10) Ministry: Israel - no missionary activity and no gospel to preach; Church - a commission to fulfill. (11) The death of Christ: Israel - guilty nationally, to be saved by it; Church - perfectly saved by it now. (12) The Father: Israel - by a peculiar relationship God was Father to the nation; Church - we are related individually to God as Father. 13) Christ: Israel - Messiah, Immanuel, King; Church - Saviour, Lord, Bridegroom, Head.   (14) The Holy Spirit: Israel - Came upon some temporarily; Church - the indwelling Holy Spirit...(17) Two farewell discourses: Israel - Olivet Discourse; Church - Upper room Discourse. (18) The promise of Christ's return: Israel - in power and glory for judgment; Church - to receive us unto Himself. (19) Position: Israel - a servant; Church - members of the family. (20) Christ's earthly reign: Israel - subjects; Church - co-reigners. (21) Priesthood: Israel - had a priesthood; Church - is a priesthood.   (22) Marriage: Israel - unfaithful wife;

Church - bride. (23) Judgments: Israel - must face judgment; Church - delivered from judgments. (24) Positions in eternity: Israel - spirits of just men made perfect in the new earth; Church - church of the firstborn in the new heavens. These clear contrasts, which show the distinction between Israel and the church, make it impossible to identify the two in one program, which it is necessary to do if the church goes through the seventieth week. These distinctions give further support to the pretribulation rapture position.[33]

The first eleven chapters of Genesis record God's dealings with early humanity in general. It was not until the twelfth chapter that we see Him working through the seed of one particular individual. Genesis 12:1-3 is assuredly the key to the unfolding of God's plan for humanity. In Genesis 12, it is recorded that God chose Abraham to be the recipient of magnificent blessing. Here God makes specific promises to the physical seed of Abraham. The unfolding of these promises is the central theme of all of Scripture.

In regard to the distinctions between Israel and the church, Pentecost explains the importance of properly understanding this covenant:

When [the] particulars are analyzed it will be seen that certain individual promises were given to Abraham, certain national promises respecting the nation of Israel, of which he was the father, were given to him, and certain universal blessings that encompassed all nations were given to him...In the development of this covenant it is of utmost importance to keep the different areas in which promise was made clearly in mind, for if the things covenanted in one area are transferred to another area only confusion will result in the subsequent interpretation. Personal promises may not be transferred to the nation and promises to Israel may not be transferred to the Gentiles.[34]

The promises for Abraham's seed are somewhat general. There are no details included here in regard to the specific nature of these promises, but they are clearly elaborated on in further Scriptures. Abraham would be a great nation, but how?

Deuteronomy 30:1-10 records the next eternal covenant with Israel, the physical seed of Abraham.

> So it shall be when all of these things have come upon you, the blessings and the curse which I have set before you, and you call them to mind in all the nations where the Lord has banished you, and you return to the Lord your God and obey Him with all your heart and soul according to all that I command you today, you and your sons, then the Lord your God will restore you from captivity, and have compassion on you, and will gather you again from all the peoples where the Lord your God has scattered you. If your outcasts are at the ends of the earth, from there the Lord your God will gather you, and from there He will bring you back And the Lord your God will bring you into the land which your fathers possessed, and you shall possess it; and He will prosper you and multiply you more than you fathers. Moreover the Lord your God will circumcise your heart and the heart of your descendants, to love the Lord your God with all your heart and with all your soul, in order that you may live. And the Lord your God will inflict these curses on your enemies and on those who hate you, who persecuted you. And you shall again obey the Lord, and observe all His commandments which I command you today.
>
> Then the Lord your God will prosper you abundantly in all the work of your hand, in the offspring of your cattle and in the produce of your ground, for the Lord will again rejoice over you for good, just as He rejoiced over your fathers; if you obey the Lord your God to keep His commandments and His statutes, which are written in the book of the Law, if you turn to the Lord your God with all your heart and all your soul (30:1-10).

Here even the promises of Genesis 12 are expanded. Israel would fail to keep the conditional Mosaic Covenant (Ex. 20, etc.) and would be cast out of her land. But the rejection would not continue forever. God would one day restore Israel to the land He gave her. When Israel should return this time, not only would she dwell in the land forever, but also she would be spiritually restored from that point on.

Some suggest that the fulfillment of this promise is in the narratives of Ezra and Nehemiah as they describe Israel's return from exile and restoration both to her land and to her God. However, the final return for Israel would be from even "the ends of the earth." This hardly describes Israel's return from exile in Babylon. Also, the spiritual restoration that is to come with the physical return has never been fulfilled. The spiritual return under Ezra and Nehemiah was temporary and short lived, while the final restoration is for "you and your descendants." Unquestionably there is a still yet future promise for Israel's physical and spiritual restoration. But even during Moses' time the details of this restoration had not been fully revealed. Pentecost again profoundly summarizes:

> From the original statement of the provisions of this covenant, it is easy to see that, on the basis of a literal fulfillment, Israel must be converted as a nation, must be regathered from her worldwide dispersion, must be installed in her land, which she is made to possess, must witness the judgment of her enemies, and must receive the material blessings vouchsafed for her. This covenant, then, is seen to have a wide influence on our eschatological expectation. Since these things have never been fulfilled, and an eternal and unconditional covenant demands a fulfillment, we must provide for just such a program in our outline of future events.[35]

In 2 Samuel 7, there is yet another expansion of the Abrahamic promises, as God makes His covenant with David. Again God promises Israel a permanent physical restoration to her land. But now we learn that leadership will come through the line of David. That leadership will be an eternal kingdom with an eternal king. Of course the passage speaks specifically of Solomon, David's son, but the phrase "your throne shall be established forever" speaks of something much grander than the reign of Solomon. This is an eternal promise of an eternal king who would come from the very line of David.

Not many years after these words were declared to David, Israel was exiled from her land.   She did return seventy years later, but there was never a complete physical restoration, there was never a complete spiritual restoration, and there was never again a king in Israel, and there hasn't been one to this day. The promises are either false, or else they are still yet future.

> Because of an anticipated future literal fulfillment, certain facts present themselves concerning Israel's future. (1) First of all, Israel must be preserved as a nation...(2) Israel must have a national existence, and be brought back into the land of her inheritance. Since David's kingdom had definite geographical boundaries and those boundaries were made a feature of the promise to David concerning his son's reign, the land must be given to this nation as the site of their national homeland. (3) David's son, the Lord Jesus Christ, must return to the earth, bodily and literally, in order to reign over David's covenanted kingdom. The allegation that Christ is seated on the Father's throne reigning over a spiritual kingdom, the church, simply does not fulfill the promises of the covenant. (4) A literal earthly kingdom must be constituted over which the returned Messiah reigns...(5) this kingdom must become an eternal kingdom. Since the "throne", "house", and kingdom were all promised to David in perpetuity, there must be no end to Messiah's reign over David's kingdom from David's throne.[36]

Deuteronomy 30 records the promise of an eternal multitude, an eternal dwelling place, and an eternal spiritual restoration. All the elements of a national entity would be present. After Israel had broken the Mosaic Covenant, God would judge her by exiling her from the land. Deuteronomy 30, a reiteration of the Land Covenant, provides more detailed provisions of fulfillment for the Abrahamic Covenant. In the same way, 2 Samuel 7 unveils further promise.

Not only would Israel have an eternal dwelling, but also she would have an eternal King, through the seed of David. Jeremiah 31 describes a future New Covenant with Israel. This is a replacement of the non-eternal, conditional Old Covenant, the Mosaic Law. This New Covenant promises eternal spiritual restoration, and forgiveness of sin, specifically for national Israel, as Pentecost explains,

> Israel, according to this covenant, must be restored to the land of Palestine, which they will possess as their own. This also entails the preservation of the nation. Israel must experience a national conversion, be regenerated, receive the forgiveness of sins and the implantation of a new heart. This takes place following the return of Messiah to the earth. Israel must experience the outpouring of the Holy Spirit so that He may produce righteousness in the individual and teach the individual so that there will be the fulness of knowledge. Israel must receive material blessings from the hand of the King into whose kingdom they have come. Palestine must be reclaimed, rebuilt, and made the glorious center of a new glorious earth in which dwelleth righteousness and peace. The Messiah who came and shed His blood as the foundation of this covenant must personally come back to this earth to effect the salvation, restoration, and blessing of the national Israel. All of these important areas of eschatological study are made necessary by this covenant.[37]

These covenants unlock the promises made to Abraham. They will be fulfilled to the last detail, including the promises of land, leadership, law, and citizenry. God's promises to the church are vastly different.

Israel was promised numerous physical and spiritual blessings, which Christ came (first advent) to consummate. Because of Israel's rejection of her King and Messiah (Mt. 12, and Jn. 12) Israel was set aside for a time, while the gentiles are grafted in to the Jewish Messiah, that the Jews might be made jealous and return to her King (Rom 9-11).

The gentiles would not be able to claim the promises made to Israel, for those were made to Abraham's physical seed. Nonetheless, recall in Genesis 12:3 that there was a blessing for all those who were not the seed of Abraham, through those who were. It is gradually made evident in the Bible that this blessing is ultimately fulfilled in Christ, and in the eternal life He provides (1 Jn. 2:25).

Israel seeks physical and spiritual restoration in an eternal, earthly kingdom, through many promises. The church has eternal life also, and seeks a heavenly kingdom through the singular promise of eternal life as revealed in all its details. The church awaits that time when the focus will return to Israel, and the church will be removed from this earth. Israel awaits the time of her judgment and refining (Jacob's trouble, Daniel's seventieth week), and her final restoration. If we would understand God's plan in history, it is imperative that we correctly discern the distinct purposes for Israel and the church. The impact of these purposes on Biblical theology cannot be overstated. The approach one takes to understanding the roles of Israel and the church will influence our understanding of Scripture to a profound degree.

8

Promises Expounded
Preparing for the Church Age

Background
The Intertestamental Period[38]

The Hebrew Bible concludes with Israel in subjection to the Persian Empire. Persia maintained its dominance until the rise of Alexander the Great, who warred against the Persian Empire in 334 BC. Alexander gained victory in just a few short years, and in doing so led Greece to swift world dominance. Inexplicably his empire crumbled as quickly as it had been built, as he became ill with fever and died in 323 BC. His kingdom was divided among his four generals, in fulfillment of Daniel's prophecy (Dan. 8:21-26): Cassander, ruled over Macedonia; Lysimachus, over Thrace and Asia Minor; Seleucus, over Syria and Babylonia; and Ptolemy, over Egypt and Arabia.

The Ptolemies exercised authority over Israel, but were tolerant and fairly uninvolved, as the Jews were allowed to continue their worship and culture. Under Ptolemy Philadelphus (285-247 BC) the Hebrew Bible was translated at Alexandria into the Greek translation known as the Septuagint. Wars between the Ptolemies and Seleucids alternated control over Palestine until Antiochus Epiphanes ascended to the Seleucid throne in 175 BC. Antiochus, the new Syrian king, took the city of Jerusalem and pillaged the temple, even sacrificing a pig in the temple[39]. This act sparked revolts initially led by a Jewish priest named Mattathias, and later by his son Judas Maccabeus. In 165 BC, Maccabeus was victorious over Lysias, Antiochus' appointed governor. This gave rise to a purification of the temple and the resumption of worship. The annual feast of Hanukkah celebrates this event.

Hellenism was also influential in creating divisions among the Jews. The scribes and priests initially were united in message, but as the priests and rulers succumbed to the Greek influence their concern for the Torah diminished. The scribes, however, remained committed to the Torah. The distinctions grew so strong that by the time of Judas Maccabeus, two sects had evolved. From the scribes came the Pharisees, and from the priests and the rulers emerged the Sadducees.

In order to ensure obedience to the written Law, the Pharisees developed a massive canon of oral laws, against which the Sadducees rebelled. The Pharisees, to their credit, recognized the reality of the spirit and spiritual matters, and thus acknowledged the concept of resurrection. The Sadducees on the other hand, were strictly temporal in their thinking, focusing as a result on efforts for the political independence of Israel. For the Sadducees the Temple was to be a cultural center, while the Pharisees began to utilize synagogues. As a result, when the Temple was destroyed in 70 AD, the Sadducees ceased to exist.

Along with the Pharisees and Sadducees, two additional sects grew to prominence. The Essenes emphasized moral purity, and, in contrast to the Sadducees, they believed in the immortality of the soul. Also they made immersion baptism prominent. The Zealots were appropriately named, as they vigorously pursued political independence for Israel.

In 138 BC, Antiochus VII sought to regain influence over Palestine, but in 129 BC, Antiochus died in battle, ending the Seleucid dynasty. Following Antiochus' death, John Hyrcanus of the Hasmonean (or Maccabean) family led Judea to a brief golden age until his death in 104 BC. Although the Hasmonean dynasty continued, civil war characterized the next years until Pompey of Rome intervened by taking Jerusalem in 63 BC. The Maccabean family tried to thwart Roman rule for the next thirty years, but the Roman grip was strong. A triumvirate of Julius Caesar, Crassus, and Pompey ruled Rome at that time. After the death of Crassus (53 BC) there was a brief civil war between Caesar and Pompey. Caesar emerged victorious, and after a brief dictatorship, Julius Caesar was killed (44 BC) and his kingdom was transferred to his grandnephew Octavian, who became Augustus Caesar.

Augustus Caesar, renowned for his reforms and emphasis on senatorial rule, presided over Rome as the first consolidated

Roman emperor from 44 BC to 14 AD. Upon his death, his stepson Tiberius ascended to the throne. He became known as Tiberius Julius Caesar Augustus. Tiberius ruled actively until 26 AD, and it was during his reign that the Messiah appeared. Appointed by Caesar as king of Judea, Herod the Great ruled until 4 BC, and it was during his rule in Judea that the Christ was born.

Intertestamental Jewish Teachings

Midrash – system of interpretation of the Tanak, in two sections: *Midrash Halaka* – handled legal texts; *Midrash Haggada* – handled historical texts

Mishnah – codified oral traditions of the Torah

Gemara – commentary on the Mishnah

Talmud – the combined Mishnah and Gemara

Midrashim – individual midrashic commentaries including *Midrash Rabbah* (on the Torah and Five Scrolls) and *Pesikta Midrashim* (on festivals)

Background

The New Testament contains twenty-seven books, inspired by God (2 Tim. 3:16) and written by nine authors over a period of roughly fifty years. The divisions of books are as follows:

I. Six Historical Books: Four Gospels, Acts, and Revelation

1. **Matthew** 45 AD – presents Messiah as King

2. **Mark** 50-60 AD – presents Messiah as Servant

3. **Luke** 60 AD – presents Messiah as Man

4. **John** 60-69 AD – presents Messiah as God

5. The **Acts** of the Apostles   63 AD – recounts birth and early years of the church

6. **Revelation**   85-95 AD – a prophetical and historical book in the sense that much of it was the history of the end times

viewed in advance. This is *not* to say that the events have been historically fulfilled, rather that what is spoken of are literal events yet to be fulfilled – history in the making. The book characterizes itself as prophecy.

II. Thirteen Pauline Epistles:

1 and 2. **1 and 2 Thessalonians** 50-51 AD – church age growth and hope

3 and 4. **1 and 2 Corinthians** 54-55 AD – church age unity and ministry

5. **Galatians** 56 AD – church age economy

6. **Romans** 57 AD – church age righteousness

7. **Philippians** 61 AD – church age walk despite affliction

8. **Philemon** 63 AD – church age repentance and forgiveness

9. **Ephesians** 63 AD – church age wealth

10. **Colossians** 63 AD – church age walk in the all-sufficient Christ

11. **1 Timothy** 65 AD – church age godliness

12. **Titus** 65 AD – church age purity

13. **2 Timothy** 67-68 AD – church age conduct

III. Eight General Epistles:

1. **James** 48 AD – church age conduct

2. **Hebrews** 64-67 AD – walking in the majesty of the Son

3. and 4. **1 and 2 Peter** 65-67 AD – church age holiness and diligence

5. **Jude** 65-67 AD – a call to contend for the faith

6., 7., and 8. **1, 2, and 3 John** 80-85 AD – church age fellowship, truth, and hospitality

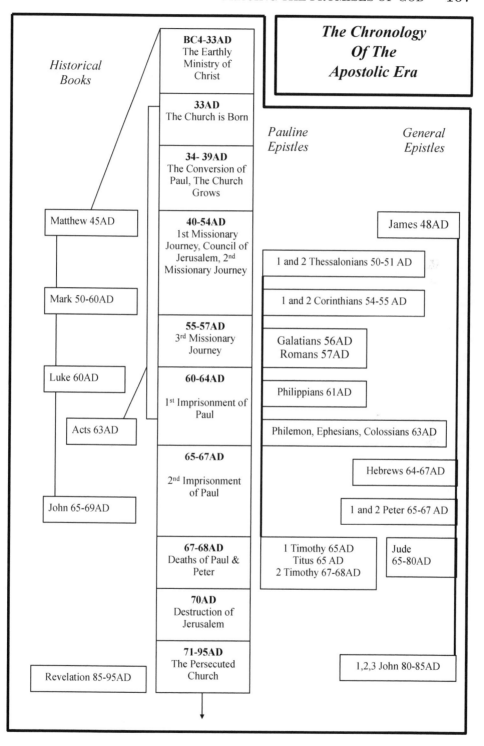

Historical
Books

BC4-33AD
The Earthly
Ministry of
Christ

**The Chronology
Of The
Apostolic Era**

33AD
The Church is Born

Pauline
Epistles

General
Epistles

34- 39AD
The Conversion of
Paul, The Church
Grows

Matthew 45AD

40-54AD
1st Missionary
Journey, Council of
Jerusalem, 2nd
Missionary Journey

James 48AD

1 and 2 Thessalonians 50-51 AD

Mark 50-60AD

1 and 2 Corinthians 54-55 AD

55-57AD
3rd Missionary
Journey

Galatians 56AD
Romans 57AD

Luke 60AD

60-64AD

1st Imprisonment of
Paul

Philippians 61AD

Acts 63AD

Philemon, Ephesians, Colossians 63AD

65-67AD

2nd Imprisonment
of Paul

Hebrews 64-67AD

1 and 2 Peter 65-67 AD

John 65-69AD

67-68AD
Deaths of Paul &
Peter

1 Timothy 65AD
Titus 65 AD
2 Timothy 67-68AD

Jude
65-80AD

70AD
Destruction of
Jerusalem

71-95AD
The Persecuted
Church

1,2,3 John 80-85AD

Revelation 85-95AD

9

Promises Embodied

The Earthly Ministry of Christ

4 BC – AD 33

The Gospels

Matthew	Mark	Luke	John

Key Issues

The Messiah Presented ----Mt. 4:17; Mk. 1:14-15; Lk. 4:16-22; Jn. 1:1-18

The Messiah Rejected --Mt. 12; Mk. 3:22-30; Lk. 11:14-36; Jn. 10:22-39

The Church Prophesied ---Mt. 16:13-20

The Timeline Expounded -------------------------Mt. 24; Mk. 13; Lk. 21

The New Covenant Anticipated--Mt. 26:26-29; Mk. 14:22-25; Lk. 22:14-20

The Rapture Promised --Jn. 14:1-3

The Holy Spirit Promised ---------------------------Jn. 14:16-31, 16:5-15

The New Covenant Ratified: The Sacrifice and Triumph of Messiah---------------------------- Mt. 27-28; Mk. 15-16; Lk. 23-24; Jn. 18-21

Introduction to the Gospels

Distinctive characteristics connect Matthew, Mark, and Luke, while John's Gospel stands alone in its context. The first three gospels handle many of the events of Christ's life in detail, while the fourth emphasizes seven specific signs in order to proclaim the deity of Christ. The first three provide a more detailed narrative of the events of Jesus' earthly ministry, while John states plainly that his intention is to record only that information that would result in a saving belief in Christ:

> Many other signs therefore Jesus also performed in the presence of the disciples which are not written in this book; but these have been written that you may believe that Jesus is the Christ, the Son of God; and that believing you may have life in His name (Jn. 20:30-31).

It is commonly assumed in modern times that Mark wrote first because his writing was shorter than Matthew's or Luke's, because much of the information in the Gospel of Mark can be found in Matthew and Luke as well, and because of apparent grammatical refinements in Matthew and Luke. It appears that Mark wrote between 50-60 AD, and while it is possible that he was the earliest author, It is highly unlikely. Most who assume Mark's early authorship also assume that Matthew and Luke borrowed from him, due to the aforementioned reasons.

Matthew was probably the only one of the first three Gospel writers to have been an eyewitness of Jesus. As one of the twelve disciples of Christ, he would have been very acquainted with the teachings and doings of the Savior. It seems most logical that his nearness to Christ would have allowed him to compose an original Gospel. It would seem strange to suggest that one who was with Jesus (Matthew) would have to borrow information from one who was not (Mark). It is most probable that Matthew wrote first and that his information came from his own eyewitness and by the guiding work of the Holy Spirit. Matthew could have written as early as 37-39 AD, but almost certainly no later than 45 AD, which would predate Mark's Gospel by at least several years. That Matthew wrote first was also universally held in the very early church. As a result his Gospel has always been placed first in the New Testament canon.

Luke clearly did borrow information, as he states this transparently in the introduction to his Gospel (1:1-3). He probably borrowed from Matthew, Mark and possibly from other disciples as well. He makes no apology for his use of sources to compile his Gospel. Even so, the authority of his writings is certainly not compromised, as he bore the authority and commendation of Paul, was a missionary in his own right, and his Gospel is cohesive with the others.

John wrote his Gospel at least before the destruction of Jerusalem in 70 AD, in part due to a present tense reference to Jerusalem (5:2).

The Documentary Hypothesis: *The Q Theory*

According to the higher critical *Q theory*, Mark wrote the first Gospel based upon the authority of Peter, and in parallel with the hypothetical source document referred to as Q. Matthew then wrote, borrowing from unique sources, from Mark, and from Q. Finally, Luke wrote, but did not use Matthew's unique sources. In fact he didn't use Matthew at all, but rather used Mark and Q, as well as his own unique sources.[40]

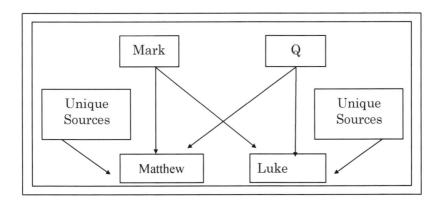

This theory seeks to explain difficult similarities and likenesses in the Gospel account, but it creates more problems than it solves. First, it assumes that God did not inspire the words of these individual men as independent, but rather used human sources to glean their information, and while Luke proclaims his use of sources (which very well could have been the other Gospels, as well as other oral traditions of the apostles which were not recorded in the Gospels); Matthew and Mark do not, which makes the documentary hypothesis a speculative leap. Second, it assumes that an eyewitness of Jesus (Matthew) borrowed from someone who was not with Jesus (Mark), creating a logical inconsistency with this hypothesis. And finally, it introduces other sources, including Q, for which there is no historical or Biblical evidence. This is too speculative and assuming, and compromises illegitimately the authority of the text.

The Gospel Genealogies

In order to meet the criteria to be Messiah, Christ had to come from the seed of David, he had to be of the tribe of Judah, in the line of Solomon (yet he could not be of the seed of Coniah, see Jer. 22:30) So it is with great care that Matthew and Luke demonstrate the lineage of Christ.

Matthew presents in his gospel the genealogy from Abraham to Joseph, the husband of Mary. Matthew itemizes fourteen generations from Abraham to David, fourteen from David to the Deportation, and fourteen from the Deportation to Christ. Not every name in the lineage of Christ is mentioned, as some were excluded (Ahaziah, Joash, Amaziah, Jehoiakim, and Eliakim, etc.) It is also significant that Matthew mentions women in his genealogy (highly unusual in Hebrew genealogies), specifically Tamar, Rahab, Ruth, Bathsheba is alluded to but not named (possibly as a consequence for adultery), and of course Mary. (Also note that 42 generations are mentioned, yet only 41 names, as David is mentioned twice, giving the genealogy a poetic symmetry.[41]) Joseph, the earthly father of Jesus, is identified as the son of Jacob.

Luke presents a different genealogy, working from Adam. As in Matthew's, there are gaps in Luke's genealogy of Christ. It was more important for the Hebrew genealogy to demonstrate legitimate descent rather than to present a comprehensive listing. Luke traces from Nathan the son of David rather than from Solomon (as Coniah was in the line of Solomon), and identifies Joseph as "of Eli," suggesting that Joseph was Eli's son in law, by virtue of his betrothal to Mary. Actually, then, Luke recounts the genealogy of Mary. Matthew traces Jesus' legal lineage and right to the throne through Joseph, recognizing God's covenant promises regarding Solomon. Luke traces Jesus' physical lineage through Mary, showing, perhaps, how Jesus avoided the curse of Coniah.

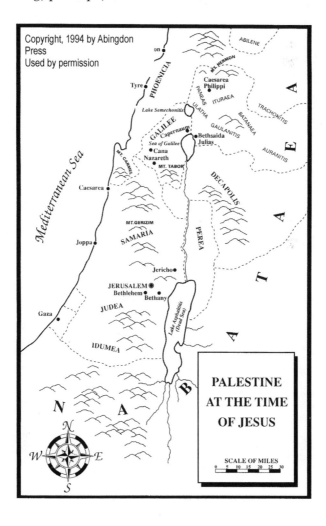

PALESTINE
AT THE TIME
OF JESUS

SCALE OF MILES
0   5   10   15   20   25   30

MATTHEW   45 AD

Matthew: The Servant King	**His Preparation 1-4:11**		1	His Genealogy & Birth
			2	His Authentication
			3	His Baptism
			4:1-11	His Perfection

Matthew: The Servant King	His Ministry 4:18-26:46	In Galilee & Judea	4:12-7:28 His Followers, Authority, & Message: Sermon on the Mount
			8-9 His Miracles: Leper, Centurion's Servant, Peter's Mother in Law
			10-11 His Messengers
			12 His Rejection
			13 His Parables
			14-15 His Compassion: Healings & Miracles
			16 His Program: The Church, His Death, & Discipleship
			17 His Glorification: Transfiguration & Authentication
			18-20:16 His Kingdom Conditions
			20:17-34 His Sacrifice Prophesied Again
		In Jerusalem	21:1-17 His Acknowledgment: Triumphal Entry & Temple Cleansing
			21:18-27 His Authority
			21:28-22:14 His Parables: 2 Sons, Landowner, & Marriage Feast
			22:15-46 His Testing: Regarding Caesar, Resurrection, Law, & Identity
			23 His Opponents: Scribes & Pharisees
			24-25 His Return: Olivet Discourse
			26:1-46 His Preparation for Death: New Covenant Ratified
	His Sacrifice & Triumph 26:47-28:20		26:47-27:26 His Betrayal & Trial
			27:27-66 His Crucifixion & Burial
			28 His Resurrection & Final Instruction

Key Issues

Background

Matthew is first identified in 9:9, and is referred to as a tax gatherer (10:3). He was also known as Levi, the son of Alphaeus (Mk. 2:14). He was one of the twelve original disciples of Christ, and he is the author of the earliest gospel account, most probably written around 45 AD. Christian tradition tells of Matthew's ministry to Ethiopia and Egypt, to whom he gave the gospel and his life in martyrdom.[42]

Summary

Matthew focuses on Messiah as the Davidic King of Israel. He traces Messiah's genealogy through David, and records His birth, baptism, and testing in preparation for His Kingdom message.

Matthew 4:17

The Messiah Presented

The Messiah's message was, "Repent, for the kingdom of heaven is at hand" (4:17), as He offered the Davidic Kingdom to Israel. Christ presented the Kingdom gospel (highlighted by His Sermon on the Mount in ch. 5-7) until that message was ultimately rejected in chapter twelve.

Matthew 12
The Messiah Rejected

The response to Jesus' announcement was a rejection of Jesus as Messiah and an accusation that His power came from Satan (12:24). This marked an irreparable sin (12:30-32), and made their rejection of Him complete. After this rejection, He spoke publicly in parables from that point on, in order to fulfill the prophecy of Isaiah 6:9-10 (13:14-15).

Matthew 16:13-20
The Church Prophesied

To His disciples, however, He spoke clearly, prophesying the coming of the church in Matthew 16:13-20. The prophecy included the following elements:

1. *The church would be built upon Christ.*

Note that Christ referred to Simon as *Peter*, which is the Greek *petros*, referring to a small stone. He then says, "upon this rock (the Greek *petra*, referring to a boulder or a cliff – the same word is used in 7:24) I will build My church" (16:18). Peter understood that the church would be built *upon Christ*, explaining that critical truth in 1 Peter 2:6-10.

2. *The church would not be defeated.*

Because of the strength of its Foundation, the church would stand against all opposition.

3. *Peter would possess the "keys to the kingdom."*

Peter fulfilled this role, being present as each people group first received the Holy Spirit (Jews in Acts 2, Samaritans in Acts 8:14-17, and the gentiles in Acts 10:44-45)

4. *The apostles would have the authority of heaven.*

Although specifically directed to Peter, Christ reiterates later that the eleven would have unique authority (Jn. 20:23). This would certainly include the authority to record the inspired word of God. As the day of His death drew near, He gave his disciples a glimpse of things to come in the Olivet Discourse of chapters 24-25.

Matthew 24
The Timeline Expounded

As the disciples were admiring the temple buildings, Christ cryptically tells them that they will be destroyed. They respond by asking Him two questions: (1) when will these things be? And (2) what will be the sign of His coming and of the end of the age?

Christ answers the first question in 24:4-14, describing wars, famines, earthquakes, persecutions, false prophets, and lawlessness. But the gospel would be preached in the entire world as a witness. That would be a sign that the end was coming.

He answers the second question in 24:15-31, as He describes in verses 15-28 the last half of the seventieth week of Daniel (Dan. 9), referring to this time period as the "great tribulation" (v.21). The seven-year tribulation would encompass Jacob's Trouble (Jer. 30:7), but the second half of this period would be unimaginably severe, and would commence with the breaking of antichrist's covenant in the middle of the seven-year period (Mt. 24:15, Dan. 9:27). Immediately after the tribulation period, the sign of His coming would appear (24:29-31). The heavens would be shaken, and His elect would be assembled from heaven and the King would return with that great assembly (Rev. 19:11-14).

Matthew 26:26-29
The New Covenant Initiated

Just as the Abrahamic and Davidic Covenants were empty without the promise of forgiveness that the New Covenant brought, even so the coming of the King, described in chapter twenty-four, would not provide hope without the New Covenant. In the Upper Room Christ teaches that His blood will pay for the New Covenant.

Matthew 27-28
The New Covenant Ratified
The Sacrifice and Triumph of Messiah

The Messiah King was crucified, just as prophesied. He was buried and rose again, just as He said. Israel had rejected her King, but God's purpose would soon become apparent. Just as through His blood Israel would one day know New Covenant forgiveness, all nations and peoples would be able to receive forgiveness through His blood. For Israel, Christ's blood would provide for the first six components of the Abrahamic Covenant in Genesis 12:1-2 (including the later announced New Covenant). For those who were not of Israel, Christ's blood would provide for the seventh component of Genesis 12:3. Truly all the families of the earth would be blessed through Him.

MARK			50-60 AD	
Mark: The Sovereign Servant	In Preparation 1:1-13		1:1-8	The Forerunner
			1:9-11	The Baptism
			1:12-13	The Testing
	In Galilee (1:14-9:50)	Message	1:14-15	Message Proclaimed
			1:16-20	Personnel of the Message
			1:21-2:12	Authority of the Message
			2:13-3:6	Nature of the Message
			3:7-5:21	Preaching of the Message
			5:22-43	Substance of the Message: Faith
			6:1-6	Origination of the Message
			6:7-30	Preaching of the Message
		Servant	6:31-44	His Compassion
			6:45-56	His Power
			7:1-23	His Attitude Toward Tradition
			7:24-8:9	His Compassion
		Response	8:10-9:10	Blindness
			9:11-50	Misunderstanding
	10 In Perea		10	Hardness of Heart
	In Jerusalem (11:1-16:20)	Servant	11:1-33	As a King
			12:1-34	His Rejection
			12:35-44	His Acceptance
			13	As a Prophet
			14:1-9	His Anointing
			14:10-11	His Betrayer
			14:12-25	His New Covenant
			14:26-42	His Preparation
		Service	14:43-52	His Betrayal
			14:53-65	Before the High Priest
			14:66-72	His Disciple's Denial
			15:1-14	Before Pilate
			15:15-41	His Crucifixion
			15:42-47	His Burial
			16:1-8	His Resurrection
			16:9-18	Before Witnesses
			16:19-20	His Ascension

Key Issues

Background

John Mark is identified as Peter's son in the faith (1 Pet. 5:13), and there is consensus among early church writers that Mark served as Peter's interpreter while Peter was in Rome.[43] Eusebius recounts the tradition of how Mark's gospel came into being:

> So brightly shone the light of true religion on the minds of Peter's hearers [in Rome] that, not satisfied with a single hearing or with the oral teaching of the divine message, they resorted to appeals of every kind to induce Mark (whose gospel we have), as he was a follower of Peter, to leave them in writing a summary of the instruction they had received by word of mouth, nor did they let him go till they had persuaded him, and thus became responsible for the writing of what is known as the Gospel according to Mark.[44]

Quoting Papias, Eusebius explains that Mark's purpose was to record everything he had heard from Peter (although not necessarily in order), and to be totally accurate in what he wrote.[45] Origen, the early church father, asserted that Mark wrote his gospel at the instruction of Peter.[46] Mark's gospel has generally been recognized as having the authority of Peter (in addition to Mark's own authority as a faithful servant of Christ), and the inspiration of the Holy Spirit. Date of authorship is between 50 and 60 AD.

Mark is initially identified as John Mark (Acts 12:12). He accompanied Barnabas and Paul on the First missionary Journey (Acts 12:25; 13:5), but left before the journey was complete (13:13), causing division between Barnabas and Paul regarding his involvement in the Second Missionary Journey (15:37). John Mark was soon restored in Paul's estimation, as he would later call John Mark a "fellow worker" and a "comfort to me" (Phlm. 24; Col. 4:10-11), and he expressed a desire for John Mark to join him, describing him as helpful in Paul's ministry (2 Tim 4:11). Mark also ministered in Egypt, being influential in the conversions of many in Alexandria, and serving as the first bishop there before being martyred under the Roman Emperor, Nero.[47]

Summary

Mark presents the Messiah as the Son of God and as the servant of God. It is a gospel of action, employing the term *immediately* forty-two times. Mark's Gospel demonstrates Christ's focus and purpose in accomplishing His sacrificial service.

Mark 1:14-15
The Messiah Presented

The ministry of Messiah begins with His presentation of the arrival of the Davidic Promise: "The time is fulfilled, and the kingdom of God is at hand; repent and believe in the gospel" (1:14-15).   This was the long awaited opportunity for Israel to receive the promised kingdom of God on earth.

Mark 3:22-30
The Messiah Rejected

As is recorded in Matthew, the Kingdom offer was rejected, as His own people (3:21) attributed His power to Satan. This was blasphemy of the work of the Holy Spirit, the unpardonable sin (3:29). The Messiah's ministry then became one of judgment, speaking in parables in order that the rejecting generation might not repent.

Mark 13
The Timeline Expounded

As in Matthew 24, the disciples ask Jesus two questions: (1) when will the destruction of the temple buildings be, and (2) what will be the sign of the fulfillment of all things. Jesus responds to the first question in 13:6-13, describing wars, earthquakes, famines, and persecutions. He responds to the second in 13:14-27, describing the latter half of the tribulation period, which would immediately precede the sign and commencement of His second coming. The application to the disciples was: *Be alert* (13:37)!

Mark 14:22-25
The New Covenant Initiated

In anticipation of His sacrificial service, Jesus teaches at the Last Supper about the initiation of or payment for the New Covenant. It is His blood, and no one else's, upon which the New Covenant promises stood. Like the Abrahamic Covenant, only God initiated it, and no one else. The promises were unconditional and assured.

Mark 15-16
The New Covenant Ratified
The Sacrifice and Triumph of Messiah

The suffering Servant of Isaiah 53 had fulfilled prophecy and had completed His sacrifice. His next advent would not be as a humble and suffering servant, but rather as the Messiah King who would install the promised Kingdom.

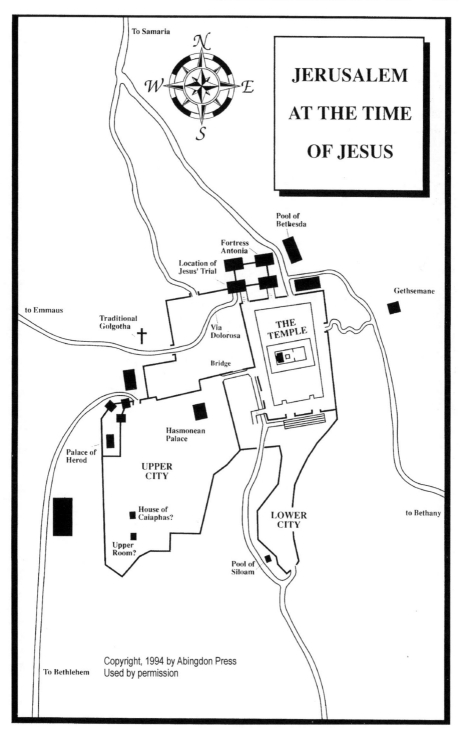

JERUSALEM

AT THE TIME

OF JESUS

To Samaria

N
W   E
S

Pool of
Bethesda

Fortress
Antonia

Location of
Jesus' Trial

Gethsemane

to Emmaus

Traditional
Golgotha

Via
Dolorosa

THE
TEMPLE

Bridge

Hasmonean
Palace

Palace of
Herod

UPPER
CITY

House of
Caiaphas?

LOWER
CITY

to Bethany

Upper
Room?

Pool of
Siloam

Copyright, 1994 by Abingdon Press
To Bethlehem   Used by permission

LUKE   60 AD

Luke: The Sovereign Son Of Man	His Preparation and Presentation 1-4:30	1-2:20 Prophecies & Births of John & Jesus
		2:21-4:13 His Preparation: Youth, Baptism, & Testing
		4:14-30 His Presentation: Teaching in the Synagogue
	His Ministry 4:31-21:46 — In Galilee & Judea	4:31-6:19 His Authority (Miracles) & Followers (Disciples)
		6:20-49 His Teachings
		7-8:3 His Compassion: Centurion's Servant, John, The Sinful Woman
		8:4-9:27 His Authority (Miracles) & Followers (Disciples)
		9:28-36 His Glorification: Transfiguration
		9:37-62 His Program: Death, Purpose of His Coming, & Discipleship Cost
		10:1-24 His Messengers: The 70
		10:25-11:13 His Teaching: The Good Samaritan, Priority, & Prayer
		11:14-54 His Rejection
		12 His Warnings: On Hypocrisy, Greed, Anxiety, Readiness, Stewardship
		13 His Willingness to Forgive
		14-16 His Parables: Wedding Feast, Dinner, Cost of Discipleship, Lost Sheep, Lost Coin, Prodigal Son, Unrighteous Steward, Rich Man & Lazarus
		17-18:8 His Instructions to Disciples: Faith, Gratitude, 2nd Coming, Prayer
		18:9-34 His Instructions: Humility, Faith, Commitment, Death & Resurrection
		18:35-19:10 His Followers: Bartamaeus & Zaccheus
	In Jerusalem	19:11-48 His Kingdom Misunderstood: Parable of the Minas, Triumphal Entry, Cleansing of the Temple
		20:1-18 His Authority
		20:19-44 His Testing: Regarding Caesar, Resurrection
		20:45-21:4 His Teaching: On Acceptable Worship
		21:5-38 His Prophetic Plan
		22:1-46 His Preparation For Death: New Covenant Ratified
	His Sacrifice & Triumph 22:47- 24:53	22:47-23:25 His Betrayal, Arrest, & Trial
		23:26-56 His Crucifixion & Burial
		24 His Resurrection, Appearances, & Ascension

Key Issues

Background

Paul identifies Luke as "the beloved physician" (Col. 4:14), as a fellow worker (Phlm. 24), and as a gentile (Col 4:11). Eusebius maintains that he was from Antioch (a possible explanation for the emphasis of Antioch in the book of Acts).[48] He remained a faithful friend of Paul, and was the last one standing with him as Paul wrote his final epistle (2 Tim. 4:11). Luke's authorship of the Gospel and its sequel, the book of Acts, is commonly accepted, as all the Greek manuscripts ascribe it to him.[49] The date of authorship was most likely 60 AD. He wrote from the authority of those who were eyewitnesses (Lk. 1:2).

Luke identifies his Gospel, the longest of the four, as a compilation of events according to eyewitnesses (1:1-2). He addresses the Gospel to Theophilus (possibly an official at Antioch), and assures him it is the exact truth (1:4). He refers to this gospel in his introduction to the book of Acts (1:1). The location and scope of Luke's activity after the martyrdom of Paul is not recorded. The nature of Luke's death is also surrounded by the same uncertainty. Some suggest he was martyred, but there is no historical evidence on which to rely.[50]

Summary

Luke presents Jesus as the Son of Man, emphasizing the human birth of Messiah (2:11), His perfection as a Man (4:13), and His mission as the One qualified to save (19:10). His Gospel is characterized by compassion for the poor and the oppressed.

Luke 4:16-22

The Messiah Presented

The presentation of Messiah in Luke points to a different event than does Matthew or Mark. Here Jesus is seen entering the synagogue, reading from Isaiah 61:1-2, an important passage about Messiah's message of deliverance to the oppressed. Jesus claims to be the fulfillment of that remarkable prophecy. The immediate response was one of rejection.

Luke 11:14-36

The Messiah Rejected

There were numerous other opportunities for the Jews to accept Him. Still their ultimate rejection came as the people attributed His power to Satan (v. 15), as also recorded in Matthew and Mark.

Luke 21

The Timeline Expounded

As in Matthew and Mark, Luke records the disciples questions, and Jesus' response as He describes false christs, wars and disturbances, earthquakes, plagues and famines, signs in the heavens and persecutions (21:8-19), followed by the tribulation period which would culminate in His second coming (21:20-28).

Luke 22:14-20

The New Covenant Initiated

Like Matthew and Mark, Luke recounts the cup at the Last Supper, symbolic of His blood poured out to seal the New Covenant. As the perfect Man, only He was qualified to serve in the substitutionary role that Messiahship required (Is. 53).

Luke 23-24

The New Covenant Ratified

The Sacrifice and Triumph of Messiah

This section of Luke includes Jesus' trial, death, burial, resurrection, and post-resurrection appearances. These narratives emphasize His perfection and qualification as Messiah. The ancient prophecies pointed to Him.

> 'These are My words which I spoke to you while I was still with you, that all things which are written about Me in the Law of Moses and the Prophets and the Psalms must be fulfilled.' Then He opened their minds to understand the Scriptures (24:44-45).

JOHN   65-69 AD

The Gospel of John: The God-Man: That You May Believe	**Presentation** 1-12	1:1-34	The Word & His Witness
		1:35-51	His Disciples
		2:1-12	His 1st Sign: Water Into Wine
		2:13-25	His Zeal: Cleansing the Temple
		3:1-21	His Teaching: 2nd Birth: Nicodemus
		3:22-36	His Witness: John's Teaching
		4:1-45	His Compassion: The Woman at the Well
		4:46-54	His 2nd Sign: Healing the Royal Official's Son
		5	His 3rd Sign (Healing on the Sabbath) & Explanation (4 Witnesses)
		6	His 4th & 5th Signs (Feeding 5k, Walk on Water) & Explanation (Bread of Life)
		7:1-52	His Authority: Teaching at the Feast of Booths
		7:53-8:11	His Mercy: Woman Caught in Adultery
		8:12-8:59	His Presentation & Rejection
		9-10	His 6th Sign (Healing the Man Born Blind) & Explanation (His Deity)
		11:1-46	His 7th Sign (Lazarus Raised) & Explanation (Resurrection & Life)
		11:47-57	His Opponents: Chief Priests & Pharisees
		12	His Hour Begun: Anointing by Mary, Triumphal Entry, Death Foretold
	Explanation 13-17	13-14	His Disciples Prepared: His Example, Betrayal Foretold, Spirit Promised
		15	His Instruction: Parable of the Vine, Command to Love, Hatred by the World
		16	His Warnings: Hatred by the World, Holy Spirit Promised, His Program
		17	His Prayer
	Verification 18-21	18	His Betrayal, Arrest, & Trial
		19	His Crucifixion & Burial
		20-21	His Resurrection & Appearances

Key Promises

Background

John is identified as the brother of James, the son of Zebedee (Mk. 1:19). He was a fisherman with his brother, and a partner of Simon (Mk. 1:20; Lk. 5:10). It appears that he was first a disciple of John the Baptist and soon came to know Jesus (1:35-39), ultimately receiving the call to apostleship (Mk. 1:20).

He refers to himself in his Gospel as "the disciple whom Jesus loved" (13:23; 19:26). Not only did he occupy a special place in Jesus' heart, he also would have a very unique ministry (21:18-24). In addition to writing his Gospel (in 65-69 AD) and his first, second, and third Epistles, he also authored the Revelation of Jesus Christ. John witnessed first-hand the future events that would ultimately fulfill the promises of God.

After the ascension of Christ, John ministered with the apostles in Jerusalem (Acts 3:1; 4:3-21; 8:1) and was later exiled to the island of Patmos, probably by Domitian (90-95 AD) for the preaching of the Gospel (Rev. 1:9). It was there that he completed the book of Revelation.

Summary

John's Gospel is distinct from the three synoptic Gospels. Rather than presenting a thorough narrative of the miracles and activities of Christ, as the Synoptics did, John presents only seven signs. His purpose for listing only these seven is stated in 20:30-31:

> Many other signs therefore Jesus also performed in the presence of the disciples, which are not written in this book;

but these have been written that you may believe that Jesus is the Christ, the Son of God; and that believing you may have life in His name.

John writes his Gospel as an apologetic for the deity of Christ, demonstrating that He was the Messiah, the Son of God, that He was One with God, and that He was God (1:1). The seven signs point to His identity.

The 7 Signs
1. Water into wine -----------------------2:1-12
2. Healing the official's son -----------4:46-54
3. Healing on the Sabbath ---------------------5
4. Feeding of five thousand ------------6:1-14
5. Walking on water --------------------6:15-25
6. Healing the man born blind ----------------9
7. Raising of Lazarus ------------------11:1-44

In addition to the seven signs, John utilized contrasts to further bolster his conclusion: light versus darkness (1:4–9), love versus hatred (15:17, 18), from above versus from below (8:23), life versus death (6:57, 58), and truth versus falsehood (8:32–47).

John 1:1-18

The Messiah Presented

John presents the Messiah as God (1:1), and as the Word, Who is the very essence of the revelation of God (1:18). He presents Messiah as Creator and Originator of life (1:3,4). And he presents Messiah's rejection as a tragedy, for light illumines darkness.

John 10:22-39
The Messiah Rejected

As is recorded in the other Gospels, many Israelites demonstrated rejection of Jesus by attributing His power to demonic origins (10:20). This was in response to His sixth sign. Mercifully, He performs yet another sign (the raising of Lazarus, ch. 11), but this time the response is even more severe: a plot to put Him to death.

John 14:1-3
Rapture Promised

Although the event described in these verses is given no name, when considered with Paul's revelation of the rapture (from the Latin term *rapto* or *raptus*, the root meaning *caught up*) in 1 Thessalonians 4:13-18, and 1 Corinthians 15:50-58, it is evident Jesus' words describing the same event. Jesus says,

> And if I go to prepare a place for you, I will come again, and receive you to Myself; that where I am, there you may be also.

This event alludes to the Jewish wedding tradition, in which the groom would leave his betrothed and prepare a place for her. At the completion of this time the groom would journey to meet his betrothed. They would meet each other half way, and he would bring her to his home. By the language of this text, the second coming of Christ is not in view. When He returns to the earth at that time, He returns *with* His bride (Rev. 19:11-14), not *for* her.

John 14:16-31; 16:5-15
The Holy Spirit Promised

In these passages Christ promises the coming of the Holy Spirit for the purpose of giving the disciples remembrance of the truth, that they might write inspired words of God (14:26; 16:13-14; 2

Tim. 3:16). The Spirit would convict the world of sin, righteousness, and judgment (16:8), and He would disclose things to come (16:13).

John 18-21
The New Covenant Ratified
The Sacrifice and Triumph of Messiah

Only God could forgive sin. Only God was perfect. Only God had the power over death. John's narrative highlights these characteristics of Jesus. He was indeed the Messiah. He is the Promised One through Whom God would keep His promises.

10

Promises Illustrated

The Bride of Christ

AD 33-???

Historical Book

The Acts of the Apostles AD 33-63

Pauline Epistles

Eschatology   *Soteriology*   *Christology*

1 Thessalonians	2 Thessalonians	1 Corinthians	2 Corinthians	Galatians	Romans	Philippians	Philemon	Ephesians	Colossians

Ecclesiology

1 Timothy	Titus	2 Timothy

General Epistles

James	Hebrews	1 Peter	2 Peter	Jude	1 John	2 John	3 John

Key Issues

The Church is Born --Acts 2

The Mystery of the Church: Salvation to the Gentiles ---Acts 10-11:18; Eph. 3:1-6; 5:28-32

The Hope of the Church: The Rapture------------------------1 Thess. 4:13-18; 1 Cor. 15:50-58

The Economy of the Church --Gal. 3-4

The Timeline Gap --Rom. 9-11

The Scope of the Church --Eph. 1:3

The Promise: Eternal Life ---1 Jn. 2:25

THE BOOK OF ACTS   63 AD

The Acts of the Apostles: The Church Age Begins	Jerusalem	Ministry of Peter	1	Commission & Preparation of the Disciples
			2	Pentecost: Coming of the Holy Spirit, Peter's Explanation, Church Born
			3	Peter's Miracle (Lame Beggar Healed) & Explanation
			4:1-31	Peter & John Arrested & Released
			4:32-5:11	Purifying the Church: Ananias & Sapphira
			5:12-42	Peter & Apostles Arrested & Released
			6:1-7	Leadership In the Church: Seven Men Chosen
			6:8-8:3	Stephen's Ministry, Arrest, Defense, & Murder
	Judea/Samaria		8:4-25	Philip, Peter, & John in Samaria
			8:26-40	Philip & the Ethiopian Eunuch
			9:1-31	Saul's Conversion & Early Ministry
			9:32-43	Peter In Joppa: Raising of Tabitha
			10-11:18	Salvation & The Holy Spirit to the Gentiles: Peter & Cornelius
	Outermost Parts of the Earth	Ministry of Paul	11:19-30	The Church at Antioch: First Called Christians
			12:1-23	Arrest & Release of Peter & Death of Herod
			12:24-14:28	1st Missionary Journey: Paul, Barnabus, & John Mark
			15:1-35	Council of Jerusalem & James' Leadership
			15:36-18:22	2nd Missionary Journey: Paul & Silas
			18:23-21:26	3rd Missionary Journey
			21:27-40	Paul Arrested
			22-23:11	Paul's Defense Before the Jews & the Sanhedrin
			23:12-35	Paul Protected: Paul's Nephew Uncovers Assassination Plot
			24	Paul's Defense before Felix
			25:1-12	Paul's Defense Before Festus: Appeal to Caesar
			25:13-26:32	Paul's Defense Before Agrippa
			27-28	Paul Journeys To Rome

Key Issue

Background

The book of Acts is the sequel to Luke's Gospel (1:1), and it continues where the Gospel left off. It forms the historical backbone of the New Testament, chronicling much of the history of the apostolic era and early church. The events concluding the book (28:30) take place in about 63 AD, yet the final events of Paul's life (64 AD) are not recorded in Acts. The best date for completion of the book is sometime in 63 AD.

The transitional nature of Acts is very important. The book traces the shift to the church age. Consequently much of the content of Acts is descriptive rather than prescriptive. That is to say that because the book records a unique transitional period we have to be careful how we apply the book to today's setting.

Summary

The outline for early church history is found in Jesus' instructions to the disciples before His ascension:

> And you shall be My witnesses both in Jerusalem, and in all Judea and Samaria, and even to the remotest part of the earth (1:8b).

The book can be further divided by the ministries of its two most prominent apostles, Peter and Paul.

Acts 2
The Church is Born

After the ascension of Christ, at the day of Pentecost the disciples were all in one place in Jerusalem as the Holy Spirit descended upon them, and they began to speak in tongues. The text here is precise on the meaning of this tongues event, as many who were making the pilgrimage to Jerusalem heard the gospel in their native tongues (2:6-13). As Peter explained (2:15-36), this was an outpouring of the Holy Spirit similar to what was prophesied in Joel 2:28, and it should not surprise the many witnesses that God would pour out His Spirit in such a way. While this event did not fulfill Joel 2:28, it did fulfill Jesus' promise that the Helper would come (Jn. 14,16). In this context speaking in tongues was literally the ability for the Jewish disciples, by the power of the Holy Spirit, to proclaim the gospel in languages they had never learned, in order to authenticate their ministries as being of God. With this event, the church was born, and the apostles would begin to fulfill the task with which Jesus commissioned them.

Acts 3-8:3
The Church in Jerusalem

The gospel message spread quickly, via the preaching ministry of the apostles. But just as Christ was persecuted, His messengers were also. The church, possibly after growing too comfortable in Jerusalem, was forced outward by severe persecutions, including arrests of apostles and ultimately the murder of Stephen. That murder was approved by a zealous Pharisee named Saul (8:1).

Acts 8:4-11:18
The Church in Judea & Samaria

The church expanded north into Samaria, led by the preaching of Philip. When it was evident that the gospel was well received in Samaria, Peter and John made their way there, and the Samaritans received the Holy Spirit (8:15). In the meantime, as Saul was busying himself with the persecution of the young church, Jesus met Saul on the road to Damascus (9:1-9). Saul discovered he was a chosen instrument, called as an apostle to minister to the gentiles, to testify before kings, and to proclaim the gospel to the sons of Israel (9:15).

As God was preparing Saul (also named Paul), He was still using Peter. Jesus had entrusted Peter with the keys to the kingdom (Mt. 16:19), and Peter would be present as the ministry of the Holy Spirit was offered to each people group. Already he had been present when both the Jews and Samaritans received the Holy Spirit, but next came something unimaginable, even for Peter.

Acts 10-11:18
Salvation to the Gentiles

The Abrahamic Covenant had promised blessing on the families of the earth (Gen. 12:3). The New Covenant promised forgiveness of sin for the Jews (Jer. 31). God used Peter to bring the gospel to a gentile named Cornelius. Cornelius believed, he and those with him, and they received forgiveness of sins (10:43), and the Holy Spirit (10:44). God had granted forgiveness of sin, the righteousness of Christ, and even the Holy Spirit to the gentiles. The Jewish believers present were not surprised that God granted the gentiles salvation, but they were amazed that God had given them the Holy Spirit (10:45).

Acts 11:19-12:23

The Church in the Outermost Parts, Part 1

Peter's ministry would continue, as the church expanded into the region of Antioch. Believers there were given the name Christians as a term of derision (11:26), but the name stuck. Derision would turn to persecution. James, the brother of John, was murdered. Peter was arrested. As the persecution intensified God was preparing another apostle to proclaim the gospel message, and to serve as a catalyst for the rapid growth of the young church.

*During this time **Matthew** completed his Gospel (45 AD).

Ministry of Paul

Acts 12:24-28:31

The Church in the Outermost Parts, Part 2

Paul was born in Tarsus (Acts 22:3) and was a Pharisee, of the tribe of Benjamin (Phil. 3:5). He also had the privilege of Roman citizenship (Acts 22:25-28). He was by trade a tent maker (Acts 18:3), and studied the Law under Gamaliel (Acts 22:3). He was known by two names, Saul and Paul (Acts 13:9).

> The usual theory is that the apostle had a Jewish name, Saul, and a Roman name, Paul...But it is best to understand that Saul's name was changed as a matter of course when he became a Christian, that the word Paul means 'little', and that Paul wanted to be known as the 'little one' in Christ's service.[51]

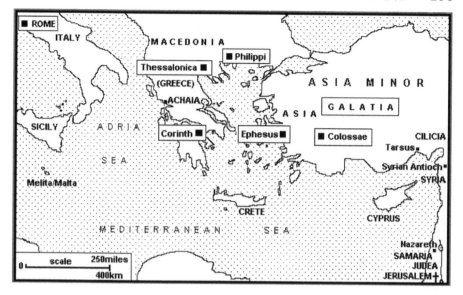

Zealously involved in persecuting the church (Acts 8:1), Paul met Christ on the road to Damascus, and was called to be an apostle (Acts 9). The church continued to grow as Paul embarked on three missionary journeys to various parts of Asia Minor, proclaiming the gospel of salvation. The first was with Barnabas and John Mark (who did not finish the journey).

Shortly after the completion of the Paul's first missionary journey, the natural growing pains of a united body of Jews and gentiles became evident. Controversy arose regarding the relationship of Mosaic Law (or lack thereof) to gentile believers. Even though Jewish believers were not under Mosaic Law, it still undergirded their culture, and many Jewish believers kept aspects of the Law by course of habit. The gentiles, being much less acquainted with the Law, had no such cultural training, and there were occasions for offense between the two ethnic groups. A council was held in Jerusalem (15), over which James the half-brother of Jesus presided. James acknowledged the Christian unity of the two groups, encouraging the Jews in their freedom from the Law, and encouraging the gentiles in sensitivity toward the Jewish heritage.

*During this time **James** completed his Epistle (48 AD).

Paul embarked on a second missionary journey shortly after the Council of Jerusalem. After some disagreement with Barnabas regarding the inclusion of John Mark (15:38-39) the two split company. Paul chose to travel with Silas, and Barnabas chose John Mark.

* During this time Paul wrote **1 and 2 Thessalonians** (50-51 AD).

Paul's third missionary journey was something of a farewell tour, and it included a two-year ministry in Ephesus (19:8,10).

* During this time Paul wrote **1 and 2 Corinthians** (54-55 AD).

* During this time **Mark** wrote his Gospel (50-60 AD).

Paul's intention was to return to Jerusalem to bring a contribution from Macedonia and Achaia to the poorer believers in Jerusalem (Rom. 15:26). He also hoped to visit Rome (19:21).

* During this time, Paul wrote **Galatians** (probably about 56 AD, although some suggest an earlier plausible date, shortly after the Council of Jerusalem) and **Romans** (57 AD).

Paul did return to Jerusalem where he would be arrested and sent to Rome. He would endure two major imprisonments there, the first lasting for roughly four years (60-64 AD). The beginning of that imprisonment is documented at the close of Acts (28:11-31).

* During this time **Luke** wrote his Gospel (60 AD), and Paul wrote his four prison Epistles: **Philippians** (61 AD), **Philemon** (63 AD), **Colossians** (63 AD), and **Ephesians** (63 AD).

* During the latter part of Paul's first imprisonment in Rome, Luke completed the book of **Acts** (63 AD).

Paul regained his freedom for a short time between 64-65 AD (1 Tim. 1:3), evidently spending the winter in Nicopolis (Tit. 3:12). It has been suggested that Nero had burned Rome and blamed the Christians. It is speculated that Nero released Paul to ease tensions and minimize criticism against himself.[52]

* During this time Paul wrote **1 Timothy** (65 AD), encouraging him to stay on at Ephesus, and shortly thereafter wrote to **Titus** (66-67 AD), encouraging him to remain strong in Crete (Tit. 1:5).

Nero continued his persecution of the Christians, and after enjoying a brief period of freedom, Paul was again imprisoned in Rome.

* During this time a second-generation believer (perhaps Apollos, Barnabus, Luke or someone else) wrote **Hebrews** (64-67). Peter wrote **1 and 2 Peter** (65-67 AD), to encourage Christians amidst the severe persecution. **Jude** (65-67 AD), the half brother of Jesus, also wrote with the same theme in mind. **John** wrote his Gospel (65-69 AD), and Paul penned his final epistle, **2 Timothy** (67-68 AD) during this time.

Nero's persecution was unrelenting, as both Peter and Paul were victims of his cruelty. Peter died by crucifixion (upside down, not deeming himself worthy to die as Christ had), and Paul, by beheading.[53] Just a couple of years after these brutalities, in 70 AD, Rome destroyed Jerusalem. The apostle John, however, managed to survive. He authored **1**, **2**, and **3 John** (80-85 AD), and while exiled on the island of Patmos recorded the **Revelation of Jesus Christ** (85-95 AD).

Conclusion

The persecution of the church had been as severe as her growth had been magnificent. The young church would continue her growth and her struggles even until today, as she enjoys the *promise* of life and awaits her hope. As the church age comes to an end in the not so distant future, Israel will begin to look for the fulfillment of the God's *promises* to her, and the nation will one day cry out for her King.

JAMES

48 AD

James (Jacob): Church Age Conduct		1:1	Greeting
	In Trials 1:2-20	1:2-4	Joy & Purpose in Trials
		1:5-8	Wisdom in Trials
		1:9-11	High Position in Trials
		1:12	Perseverance & Prize of Trials
		1:13-20	Trials of Temptation & Sin
	In Action 1:21-5:19	1:21-27	Be a Doer of the Word
		2:1-13	Be Impartial
		2:14-26	Be Faithful: Demonstrate Works
		3:1-12	Be Pure of Tongue
		3:13-18	Be Wise
		4:1-12	Sources of Dissension
		4:13-17	Condemnation of the Proud
		5:1-6	Condemnation of the Wealthy
		5:7-11	Be Patient
		5:12	Do Not Swear
		5:13-18	Empathy & Prayer
		5:19	Restoring Sinners

Personal Promises

Background

The Greek title the epistle is *Iakobou* (of Jacob), a transliteration of the Hebrew name *ya'aqov*. The Latinized name, and the one with which we are most familiar, is *James*. Two apostolic-era men with such names are possible considerations for authorship of the epistle: James the brother of John, who was the first apostle murdered (by Herod in 44 AD, see Acts 12:2), and James the son of Joseph, and half-brother of Jesus, referred to by Paul as an apostle (Gal. 1:19), and who lived until about 62 AD

The epistle appears to have been written shortly before the Council of Jerusalem of 49 AD (Acts 15) [Note in particular the absence of any mention of Gentile believers (something to be expected after 49 AD)], and also certainly before the destruction of Jerusalem in 70 AD. History suggests the author was the half-brother of Jesus. Referred to by Eusebius as James the Righteous (or Just),[54] he was at first an unbeliever (Jn. 7:5), but later came to a saving belief in Christ. He saw the resurrected Lord (1 Cor. 15:5,7), which led to his presence with the disciples in Jerusalem (Acts 1:14). Later considered as an apostle (Gal. 1:19), by all accounts he became the leader of the church at Jerusalem. His leadership is evident at the Council of Jerusalem in Acts 15.

While some accepted the epistle as authoritative, others questioned it, primarily due to misunderstandings of James' discussion of faith and works (James 2:14-26). Eusebius, for example, included it in his antilegomena (questioned books), and yet quoted 4:11 as Scripture.[55] James was universally accepted by the church as canonical at the Third Council of Carthage.

Summary

James deals at length with the conduct of the believer, particularly in light of trials and affliction. His treatise on faith and works (2:14-26) compliments the doctrines presented by Paul, for example, and gives a full and beautiful perspective of the results of saving faith. It is important to note that James is not discussing the position of the believer; rather he is considering the practice. For example, when in 2:21 James speaks of Abraham's justification "when he offered up Isaac...," James is describing events in Abraham's life that took place more than thirty years after he believed in God and was declared righteous (Gen. 15:6). James is talking about practice. The passage is similar to other highly exhortative passages like John 15 and Hebrews 4, 6 and 10.

Besides James' attention to the practice of believers, he emphasizes the profound personal promises of God, reflecting in characteristic Jewish flavor that the Covenant Keeping God who guards a nation also guards and guides his individual children, and keeps the promises He makes to them.

1 THESSALONIANS   50 AD

Application of the Gospel	Reception of the Gospel	Standing Fast in the Gospel	4:1-12 To Self, Brothers, & Outsiders	4:13-18 The Rapture	5:1-5 The Day of the Lord (2nd Coming)	5:6-28 The Responsibility of Hope
1	2	3				

			In Walk 4:1-12	In Hope		
Past Growth				4:13-5:28		
				Future Growth		
1-3			4-5			

1 Thessalonians: Church Age Growth

Key Issue

The Hope of the Church: The Rapture------------------1 Thess. 4:13-18

Background

Paul (with Silvanus and Timothy) wrote this, his earliest epistle, during his second missionary journey, from Corinth in 50-51 AD (Acts 18:1-11). Paul founded the church at Thessalonica earlier in the journey, but was forced to leave the city (Acts 17:1-10, 1 Thess. 2:15). Just a short time later (2:17), Paul writes to commend the church for past growth and to encourage future growth.

Content

Paul commends the Thessalonians for their growth, noting their "work of faith and labor of love and steadfastness of hope" (1:3), and observing that they were already an example to the brethren (1:7). He expresses gratitude for their reception of his ministry in spite of opposition (2:14-15) at Thessalonica. Even though the young church had proved faithful to that point, Paul encourages them to "excel still more" (4:1).

1 Thessalonians 4:13-18
The Hope of the Church: The Rapture

As further encouragement, Paul offers a doctrine of hope and comfort   (4:13, 18). He presents what is commonly referred to as the *rapture*. The term is the Latin translation of the phrase *caught up* in verse 17, and refers to Christ receiving the church to Himself (as promised in Jn. 14:1-3). Christ would descend and believers (the risen dead first) would meet him in the clouds (4:17), always to be together with Him. This event accomplishes several things: (1) it fulfills Christ's promise in John 14:1-3, (2) it explains the church's absence from Revelation 4-19, (3) it explains how the church returns with Christ (already being with Him) in Revelation 19, and (4) it further confirms the concept that the tribulation is a time of refining for Israel and judgment on the unbelieving world (Jer. 30:7, 1 Thess. 5:4-9). Since that period is a time of God's wrath, church-age believers will not participate in it. That is not to say that believers will not go through difficulty or persecution. On the contrary, believers will endure persecution (2 Tim. 3:12), but never the wrath of God.

2 THESSALONIANS   51 AD

2 Thessalonians: Church Age Hope	Purpose of Hope 1	1:1-2	Greeting
		1:3-5	For Growth
		1:6-10	For Assurance
		1:11	For Worthiness
		1:12	For Glory
	Clarification of Hope 2:1-12	2:1-3	Avoid Deception of False Hope
		2:4-12	The Pure Hope: The Day of the Lord (2nd Coming)
	Provision of Hope 2:13-3:5	2:13-14	Calling of God
		2:15-17	Standing in God
		3:1-5	Faithfulness of God
	Defense of Hope 3:6-18	3:6	Separation From Those Without Hope
		3:7-11	Recognizing Those Without Hope
		3:12	Rebuking Those Without Hope
		3:13	Acting in Pure Hope: Be Not Weary
		3:14-15	Be Loving to Those Without Hope
		3:16-18	Benediction

Background and Content

Paul had written 1 Thessalonians to encourage the believers and give them rapture hope amidst persecution. Evidently, some perceived that they were in the promised Day of the Lord (tribulation and second coming). Paul writes again less than a year later (51 AD, from Corinth) to combat the error (2:2-3), explaining the events that would precede that Day (2:3-12). That Day could not begin until the apostasy and the man of lawlessness is revealed. Paul encouraged believers in strength and purity, just as he had earlier encouraged them that they were not destined for God's wrath (1 Thess. 5:9).

1 CORINTHIANS   54 AD

1 Corinthians: Church Age Unity	1:1-9	Commendation
	1:10-17	Corinthian Problem: Disunity
	1:18-2:16	Humility: Godly Wisdom
	3-4:5	The Corinthian Problem: Walking Fleshly –Improper Judgment
	4:6-21	The Corinthian Problem: Arrogance
	5:1-8	The Corinthian Problem: Immorality
	5:9-6:11	Proper Judgment: Judging Within the Church
	6:12-20	Morality: Glorify God in Your Body
	7	Morality: Regarding Marriage, Condition, & Priority
	8	Humility: Christian Liberty & Food
	9	Humility: Examples of Christian Liberty
	10:1-13	Morality: Example of Immorality: Israel
	10:14-33	Proper Judgment & Humility: Matters of Conscience
	11:1-16	Proper Judgment & Humility: Headship
	11:17-34	The Corinthian Problem: The Lord's Supper Misused
	12-14	Proper Judgment & Humility: Spiritual Gifts & Love
	15	Motivation & Provision for Righteousness: Resurrection
	16	General Instructions & Conclusion

Key Issue

The Hope of the Church: Rapture and Resurrection--------1 Cor. 15:50-58

Background

Corinth was a major trade center and the political capital of Achaia. The immorality of the city was legendary, and the name of the city was synonymous with moral depravity.[56] Paul first visited the city during his second missionary journey (Acts 18:1). It was there that he met Aquilla and Priscilla, with whom he stayed and worked while he ministered in Corinth for a year and a half (Acts 18:2-3, 11).

Paul was able to observe firsthand the cultural problems that the young church in Corinth faced. A short time later, during his third missionary journey (Acts 19), from Ephesus (1 Cor. 16:8), Paul writes (54 AD) to encourage the church to maintain unity and purity under difficult circumstances.

Content

Paul alludes to a previous letter he had sent instructing them on maintaining morality amidst the Corinthian culture (5:9). The response was not as he had hoped, as he was informed of and responded to significant errors in the church, including: disunity (1:10-17), arrogance (4:18), immorality (5:1-2), misuse of the Lord's Supper (11:28-30), and misuse of spiritual gifts (12-14). Paul corrects these errors with sound doctrine on unity, humility, morality, and proper judgment – highlighted by his explanation of the temporary nature of confirming and revelatory gifts and the enduring superiority of love (ch. 13).

1 Corinthians 15:50-58

The Hope of the Church: Rapture and Resurrection

In this section Paul reveals a *mystery* (that which is previously not revealed). The doctrine of the rapture was not entirely new (Jn. 14:1-3; 1 Thess. 4:13-18), but the detailed teaching of how God would transform perishable into imperishable was new.

2 CORINTHIANS   55 AD

2 Corinthians: Church Age Ministers	Success	1:1-11	Comfort in Affliction
		1:12-24	Co-Workers in Christ
		2	Restoration & Forgiveness of Offending Brother
		3-4:15	Apostolic Ministry of the Gospel
		4:16-5:19	Eternal Significance of the Ministry
		5:20-6:18	Ministry of Reconciliation: Righteousness
		7	Ministry of Comfort
	Glory	8-9	Generosity in Ministry
	Opposition	10	Authority of the Ministers
		11-12:13	Authority of the Ministers: Paul
		12:14-13:14	Preparation for the Minister: Paul's Visit

Background and Content

Paul wrote 2 Corinthians (55 AD) from Macedonia, shortly after leaving Ephesus during his third missionary journey (2 Cor. 2:12; Acts 20). He writes (ch. 1-7) to share his rejoicing over the Corinthian response to the rebukes of 1 Corinthians (2:1-11), his joy at the arrival of Titus at Macedonia, and the encouraging news Titus brought regarding the Corinthian church (2:13; 7:5,6).

Paul also wrote of the glory of the ministry (ch. 8-9), as he had witnessed the blossoming of the Macedonian church and the gracious gifts of the churches for the poor in Jerusalem (1 Cor. 16:1; Rom. 15:25-26).

Paul concludes in chapters ten through thirteen by defending his apostolic role against a group of of Jews (11:22) who opposed his ministry.

GALATIANS   56 AD

Galatians: Church Age Freedom	The Introduction 1:1-5	1:1-3	Prologue
		1:4-5	Praise
	The Different Gospel 1:6-2:21	1:6-7	Problem Stated
		1:8-9	Problem Condemned
		1:10-2:14	Problem Unfolded
		2:15-21	Problem Refuted
	The Doctrine 3-4	3:1-5	Error: Salvation by Flesh
		3:6-4:7	Correction: Salvation by Faith
		4:8-21	Error: Works by Law
		4:22-31	Correction: Works By Liberty
	The Duty 5-6	5:1-15	Stand in Liberty
		5:16-6:18	Walk in the Spirit

Key Issue

The Economy of the Church Age ------------------------------Gal. 3-4

Background

Paul (1:1) addresses this epistle to the churches of the Roman province of Galatia (1:2), which was primarily gentile but did have a large Jewish population.[57] Paul, with Barnabas, had established churches in this region during the first missionary journey (Acts 13:4; 14:19-21). He visited the region during his second journey (Acts 16:6), and again in his third (Acts 18:23). While it is possible that Galatians was written from Antioch in 48 AD (and thus making it the earliest of Paul's epistles), it seems more likely that it was written from Ephesus in 56 AD.[58]

Content

The Galatian churches had fallen into the same error that the Judaizers of Jerusalem had eight years earlier (if the later date is correct). They were mandating adherence to Mosaic Law and teaching salvation by works. Paul responds sternly:

> I am amazed that you are so quickly deserting Him who called you by the grace of Christ, for a different gospel...even though we, or an angel from heaven should preach to you a gospel contrary to that which we have preached to you, let him be accursed...You foolish Galatians, who has bewitched you... (1:6,8; 3:1).

Paul asserts his apostleship and authority, recalling past controversies on the relationship of works and faith (ch. 2) as he prepares to communicate the reality of the economy of the church.

Galatians 3-4

The Economy of the Church

Paul reminds the Galatians that the Abrahamic promises (Gen. 12:1-3) were not nullified by the Mosaic Covenant (Gal. 3:15-18). He explains that the Law (being a conditional covenant) did not contradict the promises of God, but rather it served to shut up all men under sin, in order that the need for salvation by faith would be acknowledged (3:19-27). It serves as a tutor, leading humanity to Christ (3:24), in order that the promise of life (1 Jn. 2:25) might be given, and justification provided (3:24). Salvation has always come by faith and never by works. Consequently the walk and ultimate perfection of the believer is based also upon faith and not works (3:2).

Saving faith in the church age created a new family economy, allowing believers to be sons of God (3:26), to be united in Christ (3:28), to be heirs of promise (3:39; 1 Jn. 2:25), and to be free in Christ (ch. 4). Paul encourages the Galatians, as a result, to walk in the Spirit, and not according to the flesh (5:16). Only the Holy Spirit can bear true fruit in the believer (5:22-24). Unity and humility would be the result of obedience. Peace and mercy would rest upon the obedient (6:16).

ROMANS   57 AD

Romans: The Gospel of Righteousness	The Message 1:1-17	1:1-7	The Gospel Promised
		1:8-15	The Gospel Preached
		1:16-17	The Gospel Defined
	The Need 1:18-3:20	1:18-32	For the Gentile
		2:1-3:8	For the Jew
		3:9-20	For All
	The Provision 3:21-4:25	3:21-31	By Faith
		4	Examples of Faith
	The Result: For Believers 5-8	5-6	Free From Penalty of Sin
		7	Free From Power of Sin
		8	Free From Presence of Sin
	The Result: For Israel 9-11	9	God is Righteous
		10	Israel was Unrighteous
		11	God's Plan for Israel
	The Responsibility 12-15:13	12:1-2	To God
		12:3-21	To Men
		13:1-7	To Authority
		13:8-14	To Neighbors
		14-15:4	To Weaker Brothers
		15:5-13	To Unity
	The Progress 15:14-16:27	15:14-33	Minister of the Gospel
		16:1-16	Servants of the Gospel
		16:17-20	Servants of Deception
		16:21-27	Conclusion

Key Prophetic Issue

The Timeline Gap --Rom. 9-11

Authorship

Paul identifies himself at the outset, and he attributes the authority of his words directly to God. He wrote the letter probably from Corinth in 56-57 AD. Romans 15:25-26 indicates that at the time of writing, Paul was on his way from Macedonia and Achaia, heading to Jerusalem.

> Paul was about to go to Jerusalem...and planned to take along contributions from believers in Macedonia and Achaia...This clearly refers to the famous collection that Paul sponsored during his third Journey.[59]

This collection is mentioned in 1 Corinthians 16, and again in 2 Corinthians 8. In the latter reference, Macedonia had already made their contribution. The Corinthians also had given (Achaia was the province in which Corinth was located). Paul would return to Jerusalem to end his third missionary journey. Once in Jerusalem, Paul was arrested and imprisoned. When Romans was written, Paul was a free man. It is thus apparent that the epistle was written sometime during the end of his third missionary journey. It is most likely that Paul wrote the Epistle during his last visit to Corinth. Romans 16:1-2 references Phoebe, from the church at Cenchrea (a southern suburb of Corinth), and implies that she was the carrier of the letter.

Purpose

> The Epistle is really the chief part of the New Testament and the very purest gospel, and it is worthy not only that every Christian should know it word for word, by heart, but occupy himself with it every day, as the daily bread of the soul. It can never be read or pondered too much, and the

more it is dealt with the more precious it becomes, and the better it tastes.[60]

Paul wrote the Epistle as a substitute for his presence. He expressed a strong desire to be present with the believers in Rome but realizing the impracticality of being there, he wrote a letter discussing the very things he longed to communicate to them in person. Unlike in several other Pauline epistles, Paul does not write with the purpose of correcting any particular problem. In fact, Paul doesn't address any particular failure of the Roman church. Rather, he sought to "preach the gospel" (1:15), even to those in Rome who were already. He emphasizes that the need for the hearing and understanding of the gospel does not end once a man is saved; instead, it only just begins, for the gospel is *the* way of life.

Summary

Early in the letter, Paul makes his thesis statement:

> For I am not ashamed of the gospel, for it is the power of God for salvation to everyone who believes, to the Jew first and also to the Greek. For in it the righteousness of God is revealed from faith to faith; as it is written, 'but the righteous man shall live by faith' (1:17).

In 1:1-3:20 Paul acknowledges humanity's need for salvation, emphasizing in particular the total depravity of mankind. He notes that all men are without excuse and stand condemned. In 3:21-4:25 he provides the solution for the problem, namely, salvation by faith in Jesus Christ. Paul cites Abraham as the example of faith, bringing to our memory God's promise to Abraham that through him all the families of the earth would be blessed (Gen. 12:3). Again, the promises of God are in full view, and His work in fulfilling them is the crux of the New Testament.

In chapters five through eight he deals with the results of salvation, specifically freedom from the penalty, power, and ultimately the presence of sin. Paul explains the big picture for

Israel in chapters nine through eleven, cataloging God's purpose and redemptive work with Israel, and the keeping of His promises. In so doing, Paul identifies the purpose of the church in relation to Israel and explains indirectly the timeline gap of Daniel 9. Finally, chapters twelve through sixteen provide a detailed exposition of the application of righteousness in daily living for the believer.

Romans describes many central truths about life in Christ, including humanity's universal guilt in Adam (1:18-20; 3:23; 5:12), the implications of human depravity (6:23), Jesus' death as a substitutionary and propitiatory work on the cross (3:24; 5:6-11), the provisions of forgiveness, righteousness, and eternal life have always been by grace through faith (1:16-17; 3:28; 4:5; 5:1; 6:23), the universal indwelling of believers by the Holy Spirit (8:9), believers are not under law but are under grace (6:14), the dual nature of believers and the resulting internal spiritual struggle (7:14-25), the eternal security of believers in the love of God (8:1, 28-39), what all believers are truly called to (8:28-29), the distinction between Israel and the church (ch. 9-11), the certainty of Israel's future restoration (11:25-26, 29), the absolute sovereignty of God (9:6-24), how a believer grows spiritually (12:1-2), and the believer's various responsibilities toward God and others (6:1-2; ch. 12-15).

The epistle to the Romans also contains several key verses providing a straightforward and logical flow of gospel truth. Some refer to these verses as the *Romans Road* to salvation. There are several variations and combinations of verses from Romans that can be used together to show in simple terms what salvation is about.

Here is an example that is worth committing to memory. It will serve well those who are prepared to give an answer for the hope that is within them:

1. *We are all condemned and cannot live up to God's holy standard.* (For all have sinned and fall short of the glory of God. Rom. 3:23)

2. *The price is eternal separation from God.* (For the wages of sin is death, but the free gift of God is eternal life in Christ Jesus our Lord. Rom. 6:23)

3. *On the cross, Christ paid that price to the Father on our behalf.* (But God demonstrates His own love toward us, in that while we were yet sinners, Christ died for us. Rom. 5:8)

4. *God declares us righteous the moment we believe in Jesus Christ.* (Therefore having been justified by faith, we have peace with God through our Lord Jesus Christ. Rom. 5:1)

5. *We were once His enemies, but now are His children, and can never be condemned again.* (There is therefore now no condemnation for those who are in Christ Jesus. Rom. 8:1)

6. *Now that we are His children, we should let our Father teach us and grow us.* (I urge you therefore brethren, by the mercies of God, to present your bodies a living and holy sacrifice, acceptable to God, which is your spiritual service of worship. And do not be conformed to this world, but be transformed by the renewing of your mind, that you may prove what the will of God is, that which is good and acceptable and perfect. Rom.12:1-2)

Romans 9-11
The Timeline Gap

In light of the promises made to the believer in 8:28-39, Paul addresses the seemingly delayed promises that God made to Israel, asserting that "it is not as though the word of God has failed" (9:6). Recalling that God's promises were based upon His sovereignty (9:14-18), Paul explains that God had brought righteousness by faith to the gentiles as well (10). Paul notes that Israel had been hardened by God (11:7-10). That hardening resulted in a temporary setting aside of the nation in order that the opportunity for salvation would come to the gentiles (cf. 11:25 and Lk. 21:24).

This is the gap in Daniel's 490-year timeline (Dan. 9) between the 483rd and 484th year. This gap indicates an even broader scope of the promises of God than many imagined. God had a dual purpose in saving the believing gentiles: (1) the obvious result was their salvation, and (2) their belief would result in a jealousy on the part of the Jews, driving the nation of Israel back to their Messiah, resulting in their salvation (11:13-15).

God, in His splendid plan, would keep His promises to Abraham in two ways. First, He would restore Israel through those who were both *physical* and *spiritual* descendants of Abraham. Second, by the forgiveness of sins and the righteousness that comes through faith, God would keep His promise to Abraham regarding blessing for all the families of the earth.

PHILIPPIANS   61 AD

Philippians: Walking With God Despite Affliction	Circumstances in Affliction 1	1:1-2 Greeting
		1:3-11 Philippians' Circumstances
		1:12-26 Paul's Circumstances
		1:27-29 Encouragement in Circumstances
	Unity in Affliction 2	2:1-11 Unity by Humility
		2:12-18 Unity by Holiness
		2:19-30 Unity by Concern
	Perseverance in Affliction 3	3:1-16 Perspective of Perseverance
		3:17-21 Prize of Perseverance
	Peace in Affliction 4	4:1-3 Peace With Brethren
		4:4-9 Peace With God
		4:10-20 Peace With Circumstances
		4:21-23 Conclusion

Background

The city of Philippi was a "leading city of the district of Macedonia" (Acts 16:12). It has been called "Rome in miniature,"[61] as its people were Roman citizens, possessed the privilege to vote, and had their own governing senate and legislature.[62]

Paul first journeyed to Philippi with Timothy and Silas (Acts 16:3) during his second missionary journey, staying for some days, and speaking to women who had assembled outside the city (Acts 16:12-13). It was there that Paul met Lydia from Thyatira, who became the first Christian in Europe (Acts 16:14-15). Paul and Silas were later imprisoned there for casting out a demon from a young fortune teller (Acts 16:16-24). The two were miraculously freed from prison, and the jailor and his household became believers (Acts 16:27-34). Paul also visited during his third missionary journey (Acts 20:6). Paul wrote this epistle during his first imprisonment in Rome (1:13; 4:22) around 61 AD. Ephesians, Colossians, and Philemon were written soon after.

Content

Paul expresses the bitterness of his imprisonment, yet the epistle is filled with gratitude and contentment. He thanks the Philippians for their contributions while he was at Thessalonica (4:16) and Corinth (2 Cor. 11:8-9), and he encourages them to stand firm in spite of opposition (1:15-17; 27-28). He challenges them to unity, humility, and perseverance, reminding them of the examples of Christ (2:1-11), Timothy (2:19-30), and himself (2:12-18; ch. 3). Paul's exhortations were prompted, in part, by disunity reported among key women in the church (4:2-3). He concludes the epistle with an earnest call to prayer (4:6), to peace (4:7), to purity (4:8-9), and to contentment through the strength of Christ (4:10-13). Paul trusted in the Covenant Keeping God even when His covenant keeping was not so evident.

PHILEMON   63 AD

Philemon: A Personal Plea for Forgiveness	1-3		Greeting & Introduction
	4-7 Commendation of Philemon	4-5	For Love & Faith
		6	For Faith
		7	For Love
	8-10 Plea for Onesimus	8-9	The Nature of the Plea
		10	The Object of the Plea
	11-18 Usefulness of Onesimus	11	Once Useful
		12-15	Now Useful: As Minister
		16	Now Useful: As Brother
		17-18	Now Useful: As Partner
	19-22 Final Plea of Paul	19-21	For Onesimus
		22	For Lodging
	23-25		Conclusion

Background and Content

Paul wrote this epistle toward the end of his first Roman imprisonment (63 AD). In it he commends Philemon, a Colossian believer who owed his life to Paul (19), for love of the saints and faith in the Lord (4). Paul reminds Philemon that Paul could order him to do right. Instead he makes a loving appeal (8-9) to Philemon on behalf of a runaway slave named Onesimus. Paul's "child" in the faith (10), Onesimus was a native of Colossae (Col. 4:9) and a servant of Philemon. Onesimus sought his freedom and ran away to Rome, but instead found true freedom in Christ through the ministry of Paul while imprisoned in Rome. Though Onesimus' offense was worthy of death, Paul requests that Philemon receive him back not as a slave, but as a brother (16). Paul sends Onesimus with the letter in hand (probably also with the epistle to the Colossians, Col. 4:9), addressed not only to Philemon, but also to Apphia, Archippus, and the church (1:2). The letter serves as a reminder that forgiveness is to be given, just as it is to be received (e.g., Mt. 18:21-35).

EPHESIANS   63 AD

Ephesians: Church Age Wealth and How to Use It	1-3	The Position of the Believer	1:1-14	Basis: Father Son & Holy Spirit
			1:15-23	Prayer for Understanding
			2:1-10	New Life
			2:11-22	New Peace
			3:1-13	New Administration
			3:14-20	New Power
	4-6	The Walk of the Believer	4:1-16	In Unity
			4:17-24	In Newness
			4:25-32	In Truth
			5:1-14	In Love & Righteousness
			5:15-20	In Wisdom
			In Subjection 5:21-6:9 5:21	The Basis: Fear of Christ
			5:22-33	Wives & Husbands
			6:1-4	Children & Parents
			6:5-9	Servants & Masters
			6:10-17	In Strength
			6:18-20	In Prayer
			6:21-24	In Peace & Grace

Key Prophetic Issues

The Scope of the Church--Eph. 1:3

The Mystery of Jew/Gentile Unity in the Church---Eph. 3:1-6; 5:28-32

Background

Paul wrote to the Ephesians in 63 AD, during his first imprisonment in Rome. He addressed the letter to "the saints who are at Ephesus and those who are faithful in Christ Jesus" (1:1). This letter, along with Colossians and Philemon were apparently encyclical letters, being circulated among the churches in Asia Minor. Evidently, they were hand carried by Tychicus (6:21). Notably some of the ancient manuscripts of this letter do not contain the words "at Ephesus" in verse 1. Perhaps the letter was intended for a more general audience. Paul tells the Colossians to expect an epistle from the church at Laodicea (Col. 4:16), probably in reference to the Epistle to the Ephesians.

Ephesus is first mentioned in Acts 18-19. Aquila, Priscilla, and Paul probably founded the church there, as Paul reasoned with the Jews in the synagogue (18:19). Paul later returned to Ephesus. Finding faithful disciples there, he continued to serve there for two years. Ephesus was a challenging place for a young church to thrive. The city was a commercial hub of Asia Minor, with much of the commerce revolving around the worship (i.e., selling of crafted idols, cultic prostitution, etc.) of the Ephesian false goddess Artemis (Diana, in Latin). Revelation 2:1-7 indicates that the Ephesian church ultimately did not heed the exhortations of Paul in this letter, as the once promising church had tragically left its first love.

Summary

Paul does not rebuke the church for any wrongdoing; rather his purpose is to clarify the position of the believer and to challenge the believer to walk in a manner worthy of that position. The first three chapters explain in detail the basis and character of the believer's position, while the last three chapters deal with the applications of these doctrines. In typical Pauline form, the theology comes first, followed by the call to action.

Ephesians 1:3
The Scope of the Church

This verse describes the true scope of the church:

> Blessed be the God and Father of our Lord Jesus Christ who has blessed us with every spiritual blessing in the heavenlies in Christ (1:3).

1. *The blessings of the church are spiritual.*

This is a contrast to many of Israel's covenant blessings. While there is no doubt that the believer will share in some physical blessings (particularly during the Millennium), the blessings of the church in this age are spiritual. Of course, God blesses church age believers with many physical blessings as well, but none of those are promised or guaranteed, while the believer is guaranteed every spiritual blessing in the heavenlies in Christ.

2. *The spiritual blessings are described as being "in the heavenlies in Christ."*

The focal point of the church is the spiritual not the physical, and the basis for possessing and inheriting these blessings is the grace of God:

> For by grace you have been saved through faith, and that not of yourselves, it is the gift of God that no one should boast. For we are His workmanship, created for good works, which God prepared beforehand that we should walk in them (2:8-10).

Ephesians 3:1-6; 5:28-32
The Mystery of the Church

Mystery is from the Greek *musterion*, and it refers not to the enigmatic, but to that which has previously been unrevealed. These passages reveal two mystery aspects of the church. First, "there was made known to me the mystery...that the Gentiles are fellow heirs and fellow members of the body, and fellow partakers of the promise in Christ Jesus through the Gospel" (3:3, 6). Gentiles have joint participation (not in the covenant promises, but in the Abrahamic Covenant promise of blessing), specifically, participation in the body of Christ and the promise of eternal life (1 Jn. 2:25) through the gospel. This is a concept that was vaguely alluded to in Genesis 12:3 – "through you all the families of the earth shall be blessed." In this is evident the continuing fulfillment of God's promise to Abraham.

Second, in regard to the marital relationship of man and woman, Paul says, "this mystery is great; but I am speaking with reference to Christ and the church (5:32)." The marital relationship is an illustration of Christ's relationship to the church. This points us to Revelation 19:7, which says, "Let us rejoice and be glad and give glory to Him, for the marriage of the Lamb has come and His bride has made herself ready." The church is pictured as betrothed to Christ in the current age. Christ gave Himself up for her in the ultimate act of love. The marriage is referred to in the past tense in Revelation 19:7 (by the use of the aorist tense of *elthen*, translated, is come), and is celebrated at His second coming (Rev. 19:7,14). Note God's efficacious work in perfecting the church. In response, His bride should respond to Him by submitting to His love (Eph. 5:22-33).

COLOSSIANS   63 AD

Colossians: Walking in the Knowledge of the All-Sufficient Christ	Christ is Sufficient for Salvation 1-2:7		1:1-8	Acceptance of the Gospel			
			1:9-12	Walk in the Gospel Desired & Explained			
			1:13-23	Substance of the Gospel: Christ			
			1:24-29	Minister of the Gospel: Paul			
			2:1-7	Walk in the Gospel Commanded			
	Christ is Sufficient for Growth 2:8-23		2:8-10	As Opposed to Philosophies			
			2:11-17	As Opposed to Law			
			2:18-19	As Opposed to False Doctrine			
			2:20-23	As Opposed to Self Made Religion			
	Christ is Sufficient for our Walk 3-4:6	Mind	3:1-4	Seek Things Above			
		Manner	3:5-7	Consider the Old Man Dead			
			3:8-9	Lay Aside the Old Man			
			3:10-11	Put on the New Man			
			Characteristics of the New Man	General	3:12-17 Of Believers		
				Specific	3:18	Of Wives	
					3:19	Of Husbands	
					3:20	Of Children	
					3:21	Of Fathers	
					3:22-25	Of Servants	
					4:1	Of Masters	
					4:2-4	In Prayer	
					4:5-6	In Witness	
	Servants of Christ 4:7-18		4:7-9	Coming of Servants			
			4:10-18	Commendation of Servants			

Background

Colossae was a trade center in Phrygia, roughly twelve miles north of Laodicea. Paul apparently never visited Colossae of Laodicea (2:1), and it is best to conclude that Epaphras founded the church there (1:7; 4:12). Along with Philippians, Philemon, and Ephesians, Paul wrote this epistle during his imprisonment in Rome (63 AD) (4:3, 10, 18). The epistle was encyclical, meaning that it was to be circulated among the churches, specifically to Laodicea, from whom was coming to the Colossians another encyclical epistle, probably the epistle to the Ephesians (4:15-16). This letter was hand carried by Tychichus and Onesimus (4:7,9).

Content

The book closely parallels the epistle to the Ephesians, covering much of the same material, but with a more Christological focus. Paul reveals the *mystery* of the Person of Christ: His identity and majesty (2:2; 4:3), and His indwelling ministry (1:26-27). Paul also emphasizes the importance of the battle for the mind of the Christian in understanding the person of Christ (1:10; 2:2-3, 8, 18; 3:1-2). A proper perspective of the person of Jesus Christ will allow for a proper walk (1:9-10), while a misunderstanding of who He is can result in only inconsistency and fleshly living (2:8, 23).

In the instructional section of the letter, Paul considers the sufficiency of Christ for the believer's salvation (1:13-23) and for his growth (2:8-23), and asserts the deity of Christ (1:13-20). The second half of the epistle addresses the application of the doctrine presented in chapters 1 and 2, emphasizing Christ as the sufficiency for the believer's walk (ch. 3-4). Especially of note is Paul's exhortation to, "keep seeking the things above" (Col. 3:1ff).

1 TIMOTHY   65 AD

1 Timothy: Church Age Godliness	Charge to Godliness 1:1-20	1:1-2	Greetings
		1:3-4	Promote Godliness
		1:5-11	Purpose
		1:12-17	Patience
		1:18-20	Perseverance
	Desirability of Godliness 2-3:13	2:1-7	As a Testimony
		2:8	In Men
		2:9-15	In Women
		3:1-13	In Leaders
	Explanation of Godliness 3:14-4:16	3:14-15	The Household of God
		3:16	The Basis: The Ministry
		4:1-6	The Opposition
		4:7-16	The Defense
	Practice of Godliness 5-6:21	5:1	In Regard to Men
		5:2	In Regard to Women
		5:3-16	In Regard to Widows
		5:17-25	In Regard to Elders, Ailments, & Sin
		6:1-2	In Regard to Servants & Masters
		6:3-5	In Regard to Sound Doctrine
		6:6-10	In Regard to Money & Contentment
		6:11-21	In Regard to Timothy

Background

Paul writes this epistle after being released from his first imprisonment in Rome (3:14-15), probably around 65 AD. It is the first of his three pastoral epistles to the two young leaders (Timothy and Titus) who had served in the ministry with Paul. Timothy is introduced as an esteemed disciple from Lystra. His mother was a Jewish believer, and his father was apparently a Greek unbeliever (Acts 16:1). Paul brought Timothy with him on the second and third missionary journeys (Acts 16:3; 19:22; 20:4). Timothy's presence with Paul throughout Paul's ministry is often noted in Paul's epistles. Paul developed a strong bond of friendship with Timothy, even referring to him as his son in the faith (1:2, 18; 2 Tim. 1:2). Timothy apparently grew more and more active in leadership, serving in a pastoral leadership role at the church in Ephesus. Timothy knew of Paul's hardships firsthand, even being imprisoned himself just before the book of Hebrews was written (Heb. 13:23).

Content

Paul encourages Timothy to remain at Ephesus in order to combat false teaching (1:3-11), and to persevere, fighting the good fight (1:18). He provides Timothy with the outlines for maintaining personal godliness, as well as godliness in relation to the ministry of the church. Even though Timothy was an impressively mature young leader in the church, Paul cautions him to flee from the things which bring about ungodliness (6:3-16), and to guard the stewardship that God had given to Timothy (6:20-21; 2 Tim. 1:14). Purity and humility are the characteristics of a godly leader. Guarding those characteristics will help keep that leader from going astray (6:21).

TITUS   65 AD

Titus: Church Age Purity	Salutation 1:1-4	1:1	Writer: Paul
		1:2-3	Basis of Writing: The Promise
		1:4	Recipient: Titus
	Battle for Purity 1:5-16	1:5-9	Defense of Purity: Elders
		1:10-16	Attack on Purity: False Teachers
	Duty of Purity 2-3:11	2:1	Of Titus
		2:2	Of Older Men
		2:3	Of Older Women
		2:4-5	Of Younger Women
		2:6	Of Young Men
		2:7-8	Of Titus
		2:9-10	Of Servants
		2:11-14	The Motive: Grace
		2:15	Of Titus
		3:1-2	Of All Men & Women
		3:3-7	The Motive: Grace
		3:8-11	Of Titus
	Conclusion 3:12-15	3:12	Appeal for Visit
		3:13	Appeal for Help
		3:14	Appeal for Giving
		3:15	Final Greetings

Background

Evidently Titus was first associated with Paul at Antioch. He traveled with Paul and Barnabas to Jerusalem (Gal. 2:1,3; Acts 15). Paul expresses disappointment at not having opportunity to meet Titus in Troas (2 Cor. 2:13), but the two later joined up in Macedonia (2 Cor. 7:6-7; 13-15). Paul sent him to Corinth to assist with the collection for the saints of Jerusalem (2 Cor 8:6, 16-24). Later, Titus was left in Crete (1:5) to fulfill the same function in Crete that Timothy was fulfilling in Ephesus. As he did for Timothy, Paul cared a great deal for Titus, affectionately referring to Titus as his "true child in a common faith" (1:4). Paul wrote to Titus at approximately the same time he wrote his first epistle to Timothy, during a brief period of freedom in between his imprisonments in Rome (65 AD).

Content

Paul writes to Titus acknowledging the promise of eternal life from ages past, which is revealed in Christ (1:1-3). His purpose is to encourage Titus to maintain personal purity and purity in the church, in order to defeat the false doctrine of those who were disobedient and licentious (1:10-16). As in his letter to Timothy, Paul instructs on the duties of believers in the church and the order to be maintained. Paul closes with a request that Titus make an effort to visit him in Nicopolis (Paul would send Artemis or Tychichus to fill in while he was away) (3:12), and that he assist Zenas, the lawyer, and Apollos in their coming to Crete (3:13).

2 TIMOTHY   67-68 AD

2 Timothy: **Church Age Conduct**	1:1-2	Greeting
	1:3-5	Paul's Fondness of Timothy
	1:6-14	Paul's Encouragement of Timothy
	1:15-18	Commendation of Onesipherus
	2:1-3	Paul's Fatherly Entreaty: Be Strong
	2:4-13	Examples: Soldier, Farmer, Christ
	2:14-26	Paul's Charge to Timothy: Required Conduct
	3:1-13	Warning of the Last Days
	3:14-4:8	Paul's Solemn Charge: Preach the Word
	4:9-22	Final Instructions

Background and Content

Shortly after Paul's first letters to Timothy and Titus, he was imprisoned again in Rome. His second letter to Timothy, would be his final epistle and was written toward the latter part of his imprisonment, probably in 67-68 AD. In the letter Paul describes his personal suffering on behalf of the gospel (1:12), and his abandonment (1:15; 4:16). Only Luke had remained by his side (4:11). He recognizes that his end was fast approaching (4:6), and he voices simple requests for his cloak, books, and parchments (4:13). He hopes to see Timothy one last time (4:9) but offers him final instructions just in case.

Even amidst the seeming hopelessness of Paul's situation, he draws comfort in his confidence in the promises of God through the gospel (1:12), and in the awareness that he had served faithfully, and that he would be rewarded in accordance with those promises (4:7-8). He encourages Timothy to be diligent in his ministry (ch. 2; 4:1-8) and warns him of coming apostasy (ch. 3). Probably just a few months later, Paul was martyred. He proved faithful to the promises of God and was an example to young believers such as Timothy and Titus.

HEBREWS   64-67 AD

Hebrews: Walking in the Majesty of the Son	Understanding the Son	1-2	The Position of the Son
		3	The Faithfulness of the Son: Superior to Moses
		4:1-13	The Rest of the Son
		4:14-5:10	The Priesthood of the Son: Superior to Aaron
		5:11-6:12	Maturity in the Son
		6:13-7:28	The Superior Priesthood of the Son
	1-10:18	8	The Superior Ministry of the Son: New Covenant
		9-10:18	The Superior Sacrifice of the Son: The Perfect Offering
	Pleasing the Son	10:19-39	Confidence in the Son: Sacrifice for Sins
		11-12:3	Faith in the Son: Examples
		12:4-11	Discipline in the Son
	10:19-13:25	12:12-13:25	Walking in the Son

Authorship

We cannot be certain of who wrote this letter. While "no early writer apparently attributed the Greek text to Paul,"[63] Clement of Alexandria believed that Paul wrote it in Hebrew and that Luke translated it into Greek. Origen viewed it as Paul's work, but recognized it to have a different quality than Paul's usual style, also considering later the possibility of Luke's involvement, but ultimately he acknowledged that no one really knows but God. The Eastern church as a whole recognized Pauline authorship, while the Western church did not. Tertullian attributed the writing to Barnabas, Martin Luther to Apollos.[64] Athanasius convinced the Roman church to agree with the Eastern church on Pauline authorship. Eusebius quoted Hebrews as authoritative, but not Pauline.

By mid fourth-century, the Roman church accepted Hebrews as authoritative. Ambrose of Milan (339-397 AD) accepted the authority of the letter, but questioned its authorship. Rufinius (345-410 AD) saw it as Pauline. Jerome seems to have recognized Pauline authorship. However, he did recognize the controversy, but acknowledged that canonicity is not depended solely on apostolic authorship. Augustine recognized it as Pauline until 406 AD, after which time he refers to it as anonymous. The Council of Hippo (393 AD) recognized Pauline authorship. Thomas Aquinas thought it was a Lucan translation of Paul's Hebrew original. Erasmus denied Pauline authorship, but he also denied Johannine authorship of Revelation. Martin Luther recognized it as canonical, though of secondary importance. Luther believed Apollos to be the author. John Calvin recognized it as canonical, but not Pauline, thinking it was either written by Luke or Clement of Rome.[65] Although there is divergence of early opinion regarding the authorship of Hebrews, the authority of Hebrews was unmistakable, and it was held in high regard as Scripture.

The text itself gives us some insight about the author. He does not identify himself by name, but he seems to assume his readers know him. He was not an eyewitness of Christ (2:3). He knew of Timothy as a brother during Timothy's imprisonment (13:23). He was very well versed in the Hebrew Bible. He quotes the Septuagint exclusively for Hebrew Bible references, and he wrote in a superior style, an educated style of Koine Greek.

Paul does not seem to fit these characteristics. He identifies himself by name in his letters. He was an eyewitness of Christ on the road to Damascus. Whether or not Paul was alive during Timothy's imprisonment is questionable. He makes frequent use in his letters not only of the Septuagint but also quotes the Hebrew texts of the Hebrew Bible. The style of this letter is of distinctly higher literary quality than that of Paul's other epistles. Considering these factors, Pauline authorship is virtually impossible. Luke, Barnabas, and Apollos are all more likely candidates, though we have no evidence favoring any of those men.

The important issue is not apostolic authorship (for then we would take issue with the writings of Mark, Luke, and James, and Jude), rather it is apostolic authority. The author of Hebrews is obviously not an apostle, but his message was an apostolic one. It is in complete agreement with the writings of the apostles, and it discusses the authority of God's speaking through His Son (1:1-2). Luke, Barnabas, and Apollos all were commended by the apostles, and God could have used any one of them to produce such a work. While we can't be certain of the author, we can be confident of the veracity of the letter.

Content

The author presents Jesus as the One qualified to fill every Messianic role. Jesus was superior to every Hebrew Bible picture that foreshadowed the Messiah. He is God's final Word (ch. 1). He is the propitiation for sin and the perfect man (ch. 2). He is the perfect high priest (ch. 3-7). He is the minister of the New Covenant (ch. 8) and the fulfillment of the Old (ch. 9). He is the perfect sacrifice (ch. 10). He is the life giver through faith (ch. 11), and the fulfillment of God's promises (11:39-40). All examples point to Him (ch. 12), and He remains always the same (13:8). The author emphasizes that the identity of Jesus Christ is the key that unlocks the promises of God. To neglect Him is to neglect the entire message of Scripture (2:1-4; Jn. 5:39).

1 PETER   65-67 AD

1 Peter: Church Age Holiness Amid Persecution	Explanation of Holiness 1:1-12	1:1	The Beginning
		1:2-9	The Basis
		1:10-12	The Bearing Witness
	Reasons for Holiness 1:13-2:12	1:13-22	Redeeming Work of Christ
		1:23-2:3	Regeneration Through the Word
		2:4-8	Relationship to Christ
		2:9-10	Reception of Mercy
		2:11-12	Righteousness Amid Persecution
	Specifics of Holiness 2:13-3:9a	2:13-18	Submit to Authority
		2:19-20	Suffer for Righteousness
		2:21-25	Suffering Example: Christ
		3:1-9a	Submit to One Another
	Motivation for Holiness 3:9b-4:19	3:9b-17	Blessing of God
		3:18-22	Bought & Baptized
		4:1-11	Because it is Time
		4:12-19	Blessing by Testing
		5:1-5	Leadership in Holiness
	5:6-11		Protection in Holiness
	5:12-14		Conclusion

Background

The Roman persecutions of the church by Nero brought grave concern to those who survived. With their very existence threatened, how were they to respond? Peter addresses his first epistle to Jewish believers of the Diaspora, scattered in the provinces of Asia Minor, "Pontus, Galatia, Cappadocia, Asia, and Bithynia" (1:1). Peter asserts his authorship in 1:1, also identifying his location at the time of writing as Babylon (5:13). This may be a figurative reference to Rome (Rev. 14:8; 16:19; 17:5; 18:2,10,21). The date of writing seems most likely between 65 and 67 AD, shortly before his martyrdom.

Content

Peter writes to encourage his readers to maintain their holiness amid persecution. He first recalls the basis of positional holiness: the foreknowledge of the Father, the sanctifying of the Spirit, and the blood of Christ (1:2). Because of the power of God, the outcome was assured (1:3-5). God would keep His promise through faith. Peter also challenges the believers to "gird your minds for action" (1:13), and recounts the reasons for maintaining holiness, foremost of which was the person, work, and example of Christ (ch. 2). He includes a call to submission even to the king (2:13-20), always referring to Christ as the example. He encourages believers to maintain the proper attitudes (ch. 4), and not to be surprised at persecution (4:12-19). He concludes by pointing out that their suffering helped serve the purpose of their own maturing, and that God would achieve His purpose in them (5:10).

2 PETER   66-67 AD

2 Peter: A Reminder Unto Diligence	Basis for Diligence: The Promises 1:1-4	1:1	Author of the Letter
		1:2-4	Author of the Promises
	Diligence Due to Promise 1:5-15	1:5-11	Diligence for Growth
		1:12-15	Diligence for Knowledge
	Nature of Promises 1:16-3:18	1:16-21	Promises Seen: Prophets
		2:1-3	Promises Denied: False Prophets
		2:4-10	Promise Preserved
		2:11-22	Promises Opposed
		3:1-2	Promises Remembered
		3:3-13	Promise Coming
		3:14-18	Promise Motivation: Be Diligent

Background and Content

At the end of Peter's ministry he writes a second epistle, this one "to those who have received a faith of the same kind as ours" (1:1). Whereas in the first letter he is concerned with believers' ability to deal with persecution, here he is concerned with their ability to maintain diligence in accordance with true knowledge, and their preparedness to avoid the false teachings that had arisen. He seeks to be "stirring up your sincere mind by way of reminder" (3:1). And if any should doubt the assurance of the promised coming Day of the Lord, Peter reminds them that God's delay is due to His patience, as He seeks the salvation of the lost (3:9). Probably only months after writing this epistle, Peter was crucified upside down by Nero.[66]

JUDE   65-80 AD

Jude: Contend for the Faith	Threat of the Ungodly 1-4	1-3	The Battle
		4	The Opposition
	Examples of the Ungodly 5-7	5	Of Israel
		6	Of Angels
		7	Of Sodom & Gomorrah
	Description of the Ungodly 8-19	8-13	They are Wicked
		14-19	They are Prophesied
	Action of the Godly 20-23	20-21	To Yourselves
		22-23	To the Ungodly
	Keeper of the Godly 24-25	24	He is Able
		25	He is Sovereign

Authorship

The book of Jude was written between 65-80 AD to "those who are the called, beloved in God the Father, and kept for Jesus Christ" (1). The name *Jude* is another form of the name *Judas*, and the author identifies himself as "a bond servant of Jesus Christ, and brother of James" (11). Jude was almost certainly either Judas the apostle (not Iscariot), or Judas the half brother of Jesus. It would seem highly unlikely that the apostle Judas penned this letter, as the author refers to the apostles as "they" (17-18), not including himself in their number.

It was the custom of the day to identify oneself as being the son of his father. But in this case Jude identifies himself as the brother of James – perhaps due to James' prominence in the church at Jerusalem, or to his modesty about being related to Christ. Because the James referenced is most likely the half brother of

Jesus (Mt. 13:55), it would seem most probable that the author was a half-brother of Jesus. Due to remarkable parallel in the first eighteen verses of Jude with 2 Peter 2:3-18, some have suggested dependence by Jude on Peter's writings. However, as illustrated by the Gospels, God can give different men similar messages in order to accomplish His purpose.

Authority

Assuming the author to be a half-brother of Jesus, Jude had the same authority to write as did James. He would have obviously been an eyewitness, intimately acquainted with Jesus. He was (with James) in Jerusalem, perhaps even in the upper room with the disciples before Pentecost (Acts 1:14), and was almost certainly a participant in the Spirit's coming at Pentecost (Acts 2:1).

The authority of Jude was questioned by some early church fathers, primarily due to his quotations of extra-Biblical sources (i.e., 1 Enoch quoted in Jude 14-15, and the Assumption of Moses quoted in Jude 9). However, Paul also made use of extra-Biblical sources, citing Greek writings in Acts 17:28 and Titus 1:12-13. This literary tool does not invalidate authority. Appropriately, Jude is recognized to be canonical.[67]

Summary

Jude's purpose in writing is stated in 3-4, in which he appeals to believers that they might "contend earnestly for the faith" (3). In light of the promised "mercy of our Lord Jesus Christ" (21) he reminds believers that there is a battle for truth, and warns them of the dangers brought by false teachers and their heresies. Of great significance to the believer amidst these dangers is Jude's exhortation to respond in mercy (even if with caution) to those in danger of falling prey to error (22-23).

1 JOHN   80-85 AD

1 John: Church Age Fellowship	Vertical Fellowship	1:1-4	The Basis: The Word of Life
		1:5-10	The Conditions
		2:1-2	The Advocate: Jesus Christ
		2:3-6	The Obedience
		2:7-11	The Commandment: Love
		2:12-14	The Maturity
		2:15-17	The Warning of Worldliness
		2:18-23	The Lie vs. the Truth
		2:24-29	The Promise: Eternal Life
	1-3	3:1-10	The Righteousness
		3:11-18	The Love Needed
	Horizontal Fellowship	4:1-6	The Discernment
		4:7-18	The Love Explained
		4:19-21	The Basis of Love
		5:1-5	The Belief
		5:6-12	The Witness
		5:13-15	The Assurance
	4-5	5:16-21	The Sin

Key Promise

The Promise: Eternal Life ------------------------------------1 Jn. 2:25

Background

John's first epistle is something of a supplement to his Gospel. It is very much related in terminology and in thought. John addresses his letter to those he calls his little children (2:1), beloved (2:7), fathers (2:13), young men (2:13), and brethren (3:13). It could have been an encyclical letter, even sent to the same churches addressed in Revelation.[68] The most likely date for authorship seems to be between 80 and 85 AD.

Content

Just as his Gospel contains a specific purpose statement (Jn. 20:30-31), John succinctly states in 5:13 his purpose for writing the letter:

> These things I have written to you who believe in the name of the Son of God, in order that you may know that you have eternal life.

His Gospel was written to bring about belief in Christ, and his first Epistle was written to bring about assurance of that belief, the evidence of which was love and Christian fellowship. He concentrates on the vertical relationship with God through Christ in chapters one through three, specifically focusing on the fruit of salvation: love (2:9-10). In chapters four and five he discusses the horizontal relationship of believers to each other and underscores success in those relationships as further practical evidence of the positional reality of salvation.

1 John 2:25

The Promise: Eternal Life

Here John identifies precisely the promise for the church. This is a promise rooted in the Abrahamic Covenant, and when we consider it we should be mindful of His faithfulness in keeping His promises: "And this is the promise which He Himself made to us: eternal life" (2:25). In light of John's stated purpose, this passage reminds us that the understanding of God's promises is a significant factor in the true knowledge of assurance (5:13).

2 JOHN

80-85 AD

2 John: Walking in Truth	1-3	The Knowledge
	4	The Faithfulness
	5-6	The Commandment
	7-11	The Opposition
	12-13	The Salvation

Background and Content

John refers to himself as the elder, and addresses his second letter to "the chosen lady and her children" (1:1), either referring to a woman or a church. Most probably the reference is to a church (12; 3 John 9). The probable date of this writing is 80-85 AD. John writes to commend the lady for her children walking in truth, by virtue of obedience to the commandment to love one another (5), and cautions against wandering from Christ's simple teachings (9).

3 JOHN   80-85 AD

3 John: **Walking in Truth - Hospitality**	1-2	Salutation
	3-5	The Faithfulness
	6-8	The Allies: Brethren & Strangers
	9-11	The Opposition: Diotrephes
	12	The Ally: Demetrius
	13-14	Salutation

Background and Content

John writes his third epistle to an individual named Gaius. That name appears several times during Paul's ministry (Acts 19:29; 20:4; 1 Cor. 1:14), but it seems unlikely that the recipient of John's letter would be identifiable with those references. It does seem that Gaius was a member of the church to whom 2 John was addressed (3 John 9), and the date of writing came after that of 2 John, sometime between 80-85 AD. John writes to commend Gaius for walking in the truth, specifically by showing hospitality to brethren – even those who are strangers (6-8). He also reprimands Diotrephes for walking in contrast to the truth (9-11). It is evident through John's epistles that the proof of the knowledge of the truth is a walk in the truth – a walk of love and hospitality.

11

Promises Fulfilled

The Summation

? - Eternity

The Revelation of Jesus Christ

John's Apocalypse:
The Book of Revelation

Key Fulfillments

The Conclusion of the Church -------------------------------------Rev. 1-3

The Tribulation --Rev. 4-18

The Return of Christ With His Church --------------------------Rev. 19

The Kingdom Initiated --Rev. 20:1-6

The Ushering-in of Eternity -------------------------------Rev. 20:1-22:21

REVELATION   85-95 AD

Revelation 1-11: God's Promises Fulfilled	1			The Things You Have Seen: The Commission of John	
	The Things Which Are	Letters to the Seven Churches	2:1-7	To Ephesus	
			2:8-11	To Smyrna	
			2:12-17	To Pergamum	
			2:18-29	To Thyatira	
			3:1-6	To Sardis	
	2-3		3:7-13	To Philadelphia	
			3:14-22	To Laodicea	
	The Things Which Shall Take Place After These Things (part 1) 4-11	The Book and the Lamb: The Seven Seals	4 The Twenty Four Elders & the Four Beasts		
			5 The Lamb Worthy to Open the Book		
			6:1-2	1st Seal: Conquering	
			6:3-4	2nd Seal: War	
			6:5-6	3rd Seal: Famine	
			6:7-8	4th Seal: Death	
			6:9-11	5th Seal: Martyrs Cry for Vengeance	
			6th Seal 6:12-7:17	6:12-17 Earthquake/Catastrophe	
				7 The Remnant (Israel/Nations)	
			8-11 7th Seal (7 Trumpets)	8:1-7	1st Trumpet: Scorched Earth
				8:8-9	2nd Trumpet: Scorched Sea
				8:10-11	3rd Trumpet: Wormwood
				8:12-13	4th Trumpet: Darkness
				9:1-12	5th Trumpet: The Abyss
				9:13-11:14	6th Trumpet: Army/Book/Witnesses
				11:15-19	7th Trumpet: Kingdom Approaches

Revelation 12-22: God's Promises Fulfilled

The Things Which Shall Take Place After These Things (part 2): The Panorama

Pre-Tribulation 12:1-5	12:1-2		The Woman (Israel)
	12:3-4		The Dragon (Satan)
	12:5		The Male Child (Christ)
Early Tribulation 12:6-16	12:6		The Woman Protected
	12:7-16		Michael Wars With the Dragon
Latter Tribulation 12:17-14:20	12:17		The Dragon Enraged
	13:1-10		The Beast From the Sea
	13:11-18		The Beast From the Earth
	14:1-5		The Lamb and the 144,000
	The 3 Angels	14:6-7	Proclaiming the Gospel
		14:8	Destruction of Babylon
		14:9-12	Destruction to Beast Worshippers
	14:13		Blessing
	14:14-20		Reaping
Conclusion Of the Tribulation 15-19	The 7 Angels	15	Their Commission
		The 7 Bowls of Wrath — 16:1-2	1: Malignant Sores
		16:3	2: Polluted Sea
		16:4-7	3: Polluted Waters
		16:8-9	4: Scorching Sun
		16:10-11	5: Darkness & Pain
		16:12-16	6: Assembling at Armageddon
		16:17-19:4	7: Judgment of Babylon
	19:5-10		Marriage of the Lamb
	19:11-16		The 2nd Coming
	19:17-21		Armageddon
20:1-6			The Millennial Kingdom
20:7-10			Satan's Last Stand
20:11-15			Final Judgment: The Great White Throne
Eternity 21-22	21:1-8		New Heaven & New Earth
	21:9-22:5		New Jerusalem
	22:6-21		Conclusion

Key Fulfillments

Background

By this time John was the last surviving apostle. While he had been spared martyrdom, he still suffered exile at the island of Patmos (1:9), at the hands of the emperor Domitian. It was during this exile, between 85-95 AD, that he recorded the last component of God's revealed word, the Revelation of Jesus Christ. It is evident that John was uniquely set apart for the special task of recording this Revelation (Jn. 21:20-24).

The book is also unique in several ways. It is, for example, the only book that offers a blessing to those who read, hear, and heed the words of the prophecy (1:3; 22:7). Likewise it pronounces a unique curse for adding to or taking away from the words (22:18-19). This blessing and curse underscores the importance of taking every word at face value, and handling each one with a literal grammatical-historical hermeneutic. Understanding the words in this straightforward way, the reader will recognize the simplicity of the message of the final fulfillments of the promises of God.

Summary

The outline for the book is mentioned in the commission of John: "Write therefore the things which you have seen, and the things which are, and the things which shall take place after these things" (Rev. 1:19).

Revelation 1
The Things Which You Have Seen

John records a stunning vision of the Messiah King, who commissions the writing.

Revelation 2-3
The Things Which Are

Revelation 1-3
The Conclusion of the Church

These letters are written to actual churches in Asia Minor. To Ephesus: Christ commends their perseverance, yet rebukes them for leaving their first love (2:1-7). To Smyrna: He encourages them to overcome during times of tribulation (2:8-11). To Pergamum: He commends their faithfulness to Him, but rebukes their tolerance of false teaching and calls them to repentance (2:12-17). To Thyatira: as to Pergamum, He commends their faithfulness, while rebuking their tolerance for false teaching (specifically the prophetess, Jezebel), and concludes by encouraging them to persevere (2:18-29). To Sardis: He partially commends their deeds but rebukes them for being dead, and challenges them to repentance (3:1-6). To Philadelphia: He offers no rebuke, but only commendation and a call to perseverance (3:7-13). Finally, to Laodicea: He warns them of the consequences for being lukewarm. This is a church comprised of believers who are so arrogant and unfaithful that they are described as poor, wretched, and miserable (3:14-22).

These letters provide the last mention of the church until she appears in heaven returning with Christ, pure and refined (Rev. 19:11-16). The rapture removes the church from earth before the Day of the Lord begins (Jn. 14:3; 1 Thess. 4:13-18; 1 Cor. 15:50-58), and so the church will not participate in the time designated *Jacob's Trouble* (Jer. 30:7).

Revelation 4-22
The Things Which Shall Take Place After These Things

Revelation 4-18
The Tribulation: Jacob's Trouble

John records the events that will take place during Jacob's Trouble (Jer. 30:7), and Daniel's seventieth week (Dan. 9:24-27), the last half of which Christ called the great tribulation (Mt. 24:15-31). The events have the twofold purpose of refining Israel for her coming King, and judging the world for its wickedness. The judgments include the seven seals, seven trumpets, seven angels, and the seven bowls of wrath. Daniel's fourth kingdom (the Roman Confederacy) is judged for evils comparable to those of Babylon (ch. 17-18). Even in times of the most severe judgment, God protects Israel (ch. 12) and gives opportunity to repent (14:1-5).

Revelation 19
The Return of Christ with His Church

Christ returns triumphantly and with the church (19:11-19). He judges the antichrist and his false prophet with those who had received antichrist's mark and who worshipped him (19:20-21).

Revelation 20:1-6
The Kingdom Initiated

In keeping the Davidic Covenant (2 Sam. 7), Christ returns to the earth. After imprisoning Satan (20:1-3), He takes His place on the throne of David, presiding for one thousand years over the Kingdom that Ezekiel described (Ezek. 37-48). From this point the Messiah King will soon usher in eternity

Revelation 20:7-22:21

The Ushering-in of Eternity

After the release of Satan and his final failed rebellion and judgment (20:7-10), Christ judges at the Great White Throne all whose names were not written in the book of life, according to their deeds (20:12, 15). Those deeds, of course, are unsatisfactory to God because faith is required to please Him (Jn. 3:16; Heb. 11:6). All those who are judged are cast into the lake of fire (20:15).

God does away with heaven and earth, replacing them with a new heaven and earth (20:11; 21:1) never to be stained by sin. Meanwhile the city of New Jerusalem (presumably replacing the old one) comes down out of heaven (21:2-21), and becomes the center of worship for the Messiah King (21:2-22:5). These things mark the fulfillment of God's promises to Abraham (Gen. 12:1-3) of a great nation and worldwide blessing; to David (2 Sam. 7) of an eternal kingdom; and of the New Covenant (Jer. 31) which promised an eternal physical and spiritual restoration of Israel, accompanied by the forgiveness of their sins.

The Revelation concludes with an assurance of Jesus' qualification and capability to fulfill the covenants (22:12-13, 16) and with a promise that He would indeed return (22:20). God keeps His promises always, to the praise of His glory.

And let the one who is thirsty come; let the one who wishes take the water of life without cost.

Revelation 22:17

Notes

[1] Ex. 17:14, 24:4, 34:27, Num. 33:1-2, Deut. 31:9.

[2] Josh 1:8, 8:31, 1 Kin. 2:3, 2 Kin. 21:8, Ezra 6:18, Neh. 13:1, Dan. 9:11-13, Mal. 4:4.

[3] Mt. 8:4, 19:7-8, Mk. 1:44, 7:10, 10:3-5, 12:26, Lk. 5:14, 16:29-31, 24:44, Jn. 5:45-46, 7:19-22.

[4] Gleason Archer, *A Survey of Old Testament Introduction* (Chicago, IL: Moody Press, 1994), 113.

[5] Jamieson, Fausset, and Brown, *Bible Commentary, Job-Malachi,* (Peabody, MA: Hendrickson, 2002), viii.

[6] Gleason Archer, *The Encyclopedia of Bible Difficulties* (Grand Rapids, MI: Zondervan, 1982), 236.

[7] Jamieson, Fausset, and Brown, *Bible Commentary, Job-Malachi,* (Peabody, MA: Hendrickson, 2002), 86.

[8] Keil & Delitzsch , *Commentary on the Old Testament, Jeremiah and Lamentations* (Peabody, MA: Hendrickson, 2001), 232.

[9] Robert Hubbard Jr, *First and Second Kings* (Chicago, IL: Moody Press, 1991), 11.

[10] Samuel Schultz, *The Old Testament Speaks* (New York: Harper & Row, 1970), 286.

[11] Keil & Delitzsch, *Commentary on the Old Testament, Psalms* (Peabody, MA: Hendrickson, 2001), 10.

[12] Derek Kidner, *Psalms 1-72.* (London: Intervasity Press, 1973), 37-43.

[13] Gleason Archer, *A Survey of Old Testament Introduction* (Chicago, IL: Moody Press, 1994), 335.

[14] John Walvoord, *Major Bible Prophecies* (Grand Rapids, MI: Zondervan, 1991), 271.

[15] Dwight Pentecost, *Things to Come* (Grand Rapids, MI: Zondervan, 1958), 230.

[16] *Ryrie Study Bible* notes, 1353.

[17] Merrill Unger, *The New Unger's Bible Dictionary* (Chicago, IL: Moody Press,1988), 925.

[18] Keil & Delitzsch, *Commentary on the Old Testament*, Isaiah (Peabody, MA: Hendrickson, 2001), 22.

[19] Gleason Archer, *A Survey of Old Testament Introduction* (Chicago, IL: Moody Press, 1994), 391.

[20] R.K. Harrison, *Jeremiah and Lamentations* (Downers Grove, IL: Intervarsity Press, 1973), 195.

[21] Gleason Archer, *A Survey of Old Testament Introduction* (Chicago, IL: Moody Press, 1994), 413.

[22] Keil & Delitzsch, *Commentary on the Old Testament*, *Ezekiel* (Peabody, MA: Hendrickson, 2001), 507.

[23] Ibid.

[24] Jamieson, Fausset, and Brown, *Bible Commentary, Job-Malachi*, (Peabody, MA: Hendrickson, 2002), 429.

[25] An alternate view recognizes the decree as referring to Ezra 7, which would, according to the sun calendar, complete the 483 years at 26 AD, or according to the lunar calendar, end at roughly 20 AD. Either possibility would be an accurate fulfillment of the stated prophecy and timeline.

[26] H.B. Hackett, ed., *Smith's Dictionary of the Bible* (Boston, MA: Houghton Mifflin and Co., 1892), 2009, and Josephus, 11:6:1.

[27] Thomas Constable, *Notes on Esther*, (Dallas, TX: Sonic Light, 2004), 1.

[28] Gleason Archer, *A Survey of Old Testament Introduction* (Chicago, IL: Moody Press, 1994), 479.

[29] Arnold Fruchtenbaum, *Israelology* (Tustin, CA: Ariel Ministries Press, 1993), 3.

[30] Charles Ryrie, *Basic Theology* (Wheaton, IL: Victor Books, 1989), 397.

[31]Lewis Sperry Chafer, *Systematic Theology, Vol. 4* (Grand Rapids, MI: Kregel, 1993), 27.

[32] Pentecost, 65.

[33] Ibid., 201-202.

[34] Ibid., 72-73.

[35] Ibid., 98-99.

[36] Ibid., 114-115.

[37] Ibid., 128.

[38] Josephus; Cecil Roth; and *The Columbia Encyclopedia.*

[39] Josephus, 12:5:4.

[40] Adapted from chart: Robert Stein, *The Synoptic Problem* (Grand Rapids, MI: Baker, 1987), 274.

[41] A.T. Robertson, *A Harmony of the Gospels* (New York, NY: Harper and Row, 1950), 261.

[42] W. Grinton Berry, *Foxe's Book of Martyrs* (Old Tappan, NJ: Power Books), 9.

[43] AT Robertson, *Word Pictures In the New Testament Matthew and Mark* (Nashville, TN: Broadman, 1931), 249.

[44] G.A. Williamson, ed., Eusebius, *The History of the Church* (New York, NY: Barnes and Noble Books, 1995), 88.

[45] Ibid., 152.

[46] Ibid., 265.

[47] *Foxe's Book of Martyrs,* 7.

[48] Eusebius, 109.

[49] AT Robertson, *Word Pictures In the New Testament: Luke* (Nashville, TN: Broadman, 1931), ix.

[50] Unger, 788, and *Smith's Dictionary of the Bible,* 1693.

[51] Unger, 968.

[52] Homer Kent, *The Pastoral Epistles* (Salem, WI: Sheffield Publishing Co., 1993), 243.

[53] Eusebius, 104, and *Foxe's Book of Martyrs*, 13.

[54] Eusebius, 72.

[55] Unger, 650.

[56] Mal Couch, *A Bible Handbook to the Acts of the Apostles* (Grand Rapids, MI: Kregel, 1999), 345.

[57] J.B. Lightfoot, *St. Paul's Epistles, St. Paul's Epistle to the Galatians* (Peabody, MA: Hendrickson, 1995), 9.

[58] F.F.Bruce, "Galatian Problems. 4. The Date of the Epistle," *Bulletin of the John Rylands Library* 54 (Spring 1972): 251.

[59] Robert Picirilli, *Paul the Apostle* (Chicago, IL: Moody Press, 1986), 156.

[60] Martin Luther, *Commentary on Romans* (Grand Rapids, MI: Kregel, 1976), Preface.

[61] W. Hendriksen, *The Epistle to the Philippians* (Banner of Truth, 1963), 7.

[62] Unger, 1002.

[63] AT Robertson, *Word Pictures In the New Testament: John & Hebrews* (Nashville, TN: Broadman, 1931), 329.

[64] Merrill Tenney, *New Testament Survey* (Grand Rapids, MI: Eerdmans, 1985), 358-359.

[65] F.F. Bruce, *The Canon of Scripture* (Downers Grove, IL: Intervarsity Press, 1988).

[66] Eusebius, 104, and *Foxe's Book of Martyrs*, 13.

[67] Recognized at the Third Council of Carthage, AD 397.

[68] AT Robertson, *Word Pictures In the New Testament: General Epistles* (Nashville, TN: Broadman, 1931), 201.